LESSONS FROM A LIFE COACH

8 Basic Steps to Change!

A practical workbook–Not to change who we are

To change the things within that hold us back–
From being all that we can be

Sherianne Angel

First published 2014

ISBN 978-0-9831447-2-4

Cover design by Maari Casey
Text design by Bookwrights

Dedicated to

Daron who taught me what true giving is all about

Contents

Introduction

What is **life coaching**?

"Life coaching" is a set of down to earth, practical ideas for people of all ages, backgrounds and abilities which is meant to help anyone achieve his or her fullest potential. Life coaching is not designed to cure significant mental illness. Instead, life coaching focuses on the important and common issues faced by most people as they journey through life. Life coaching is for anyone who dreams of a life full of joy and authenticity. You might never have thought that you could achieve meaningfulness and lasting happiness, but life coaching can work for you! This book will show you how.

What am I hoping to share with you in this book?

The purpose of this book is to help you acquire the building blocks which you will need to achieve self-growth. The first layer of these blocks is self-awareness. All of us require self-awareness as the first, most essential tool which we will use to create a life of meaning. We often feel that we are in close touch with ourselves and therefore have self-awareness, but in fact the majority of us have not yet attained this level. As a result, we tend to make the same mistakes over and over again while wondering what we are doing wrong and why we aren't truly happy and fulfilled. Achieving self-awareness requires time and effort, but you can do it!

As you read, you will notice that this book is written as if you and I were having a friendly conversation. Just like "real" sessions between a life coach and his or her client, you and I will join together to help you begin on a new direction. My own journey began with a quest to heal myself and I believe that healing inevitably requires the vast creative power of the larger universe, a power that is beyond our selves and even beyond our imaginations. It is my feeling that *all of us are here for a reason*, that our purpose matters and that all of us can bring remarkable change and goodness into the world. There is nothing in this philosophy that requires you to be of any particular faith or background. Instead, let us accept that you are both powerful and open to change as we journey together.

Your potential is limitless!

Each chapter of this book is structured in the following way:

First: You will find a discussion about the issue which reflects the title of each chapter.

Second: You will see a box which outlines strategies and evaluation tips that describe the stages which will help you bring about changes in your life. This is meant to guide you through your work step by step. I suggest you practice one strategy at a time for at least one week, before moving to the next strategy. You should find this process to be practical, simple, and reachable.

Third: Homework concludes each lesson and is designed to help you reinforce your understanding of the theme.

As you go along, you will learn to recognize your own self-defeating patterns and you will begin to use new ways of responding to old issues.

Let's get started!

We so often blame other people for our unhappiness. We mistakenly believe that if *other* people who are important to us change, *then* we'll be happy. But the truth is that while we do have the power to change ourselves, we don't have the power to change others.

You can transform yourself but you cannot change others.

Other people must take on their own journeys, just like you have taken on yours. However, the changes that you make will undoubtedly influence others, creating an atmosphere of greater openness and possibilities.

By the time you reach the end of this book, I hope you will understand yourself better, have more clarity about your unique challenges in life, and be ready to make some simple changes. **This journey is yours and is utterly unique in the world.**

The first chapter of this book covers how your earliest experiences, family, environment, and personality continue to have profound effects on you as an adult. The following chapters go on to discuss basic issues which are fundamental to making changes **now**.

How should you approach this book for maximum benefit?

First, I suggest that you read this book straight through the first time. Then, come back to the lesson that seems to speak loudest to you. Do the homework and focus on practicing the strategies contained in them whenever the opportunity arises. Give yourself enough time (a minimum of one week per lesson) to become familiar with each strategy before going on to the next lesson. Each lesson is meant to be a building block to the next. The combined lessons form a strong foundation. In this volume, we introduce seven lessons, and an eighth which encourages you to rejoice in your success by celebrating your victories.

This is a project that requires patience! This process can't be rushed.

You are important and deserve to enjoy what you do as you go along. **Be sure, as you work, to set realistic expectations** for yourself and don't let small fall backs that you perceive as failures get in your way! Rather, pick yourself up move forward again. Fall backs are a natural function in the process of personal growth. It is often a time when you consolidate all you have learned before moving forward again.

If you find it easier to work with others, go ahead and include a trusted friend or a small group of like-minded people to work with. This is your process and you are free to decide how to make it work best for you.

Lesson 1

Let's Grow

Anatomy of Self Growth

Imagine a situation in which you plant a sapling in a small container. You set the container in the sun, you water the sapling, and sometimes give it fertilizer. Over time, the sapling grows and brings forth new leaves and branches. But eventually the tree will outgrow the original container. What happens if you don't transplant the tree? It won't matter if you continue to water the tree, and it won't matter if you give it fertilizer, talk to it, or make sure it gets enough sun. Eventually, even with plenty of loving care, the tree will fail to grow and eventually it will die. This is what happens with people as well.

If we don't open ourselves up to opportunities for personal growth we can't achieve our fullest potential.

In order to live rich and full lives, we are challenged to uproot ourselves psychologically, in search of a healthier place to become our entire selves. The goal of personal growth is to become ever closer to the best of who we can be, *to see this as a process,* and to allow ourselves to embrace the challenges that we encounter along the way.

What is self growth? What does it actually look like? To really understand what self growth is, we need to start at the beginning...

We all come into the world with inborn character traits. We seem to be naturally equipped with certain strengths and areas of challenge. For example, some babies are outgoing and smiley while others are shy and very sensitive. Both strengths and weaknesses form the basis of who we can be and provide the raw materials for our later personality development. As we mature, our environment (the world around us and the people who are most important to us) impact who we are, how we feel about ourselves, and how we interact with each other and the wider world. It is from the result of interactions with our environment that very young children can begin to grow anxious and identify in themselves negative attributes such as unattractiveness or a lack of worth.

Once a young child begins to feel that he or she is not worthy, this concept takes on meaning and the child will believe that this is true.

In the same way, if a young child is consistently taught that she is wonderful and is the center of the universe, she will believe that and take on behaviors which reflect her belief that she is more important than other people.

Even if we were fortunate to be raised in a happy, relatively uncomplicated family, there is still a lot of room for personal growth. In fact, this is true even more so since you can launch yourself forward from a solid foundation.

Since very young children are not yet capable of questioning this early information, they will not only accept what they've heard as truth, but they will also behave as if what they have heard is truth. As we develop, we automatically form a web of information from everything that we observe and learn about ourselves and others. This web of information is underneath the surface of our awareness and is built, over time, throughout our earliest years. This is where our first impressions of the world are formed. It becomes our first point of reference.

We use this web of information to guide us to understand who we are, what we feel, what we need, and who we want to be. Very young children do not know that they are unconsciously forming this perception of the world. The information in this web drives behavior and feelings but the surprising thing is that what is found in this web is not necessarily what is good for you. The information is simply what's been learned. The great news here is that because it has been learned, it can be un-learned!

We can also be dramatically and negatively affected by traumatic events that happen to us later in life. Traumatic events impinge on individuals differently but very often the distressing after effects linger, creating changes that can lead to problems for us personally or in our relationships. It takes time to work through and process the disturbing events until we are able to heal and learn to feel safe and whole once again.

This book is all about changing those things which you've incorporated into the web of information that obstructs your natural ability for healthy emotional and psychological growth. The place to start is with self-awareness. Self awareness is a state of being in tune with your thoughts and emotions, knowing how you are feeling, and reacting in a given way at any particular moment. It is a place from which you can clearly perceive the effects of your behaviors on others. Without self awareness, your behavior, thoughts, and feelings can seem out of your control and you will have much more difficulty understanding why you have behaved as you have. Since we are only rarely taught how to be self aware when we are children, it is often the job of adulthood to learn what self awareness is and how to master it.

This is where personal growth and self awareness becomes so important.

Ordinarily, people are consumed with simple day to day tasks without giving much thought to understanding themselves and others in a deeper, more emotional way. To better understand ourselves and others, it is *vital* that we do more than take care of what is superficial in our lives.

When we grow as people we then have the chance to connect more intimately with others.

When we grow, we know ourselves better, understand the impact of our behavior on others, learn from our experience, and generally feel happier and more balanced.

Each of us has gone through a unique childhood. Even if you have an identical twin, you have grown up separately and on your own. People who took care of you responded to you as a unique individual and because of that you have your own personal perception of the world and therefore your own personal set of issues which comes out of your web of information.

When we feel stuck, it is usually within this "set of issues" that the problem lies and where a solution can be found.

Perhaps your "set of issues" is about a lack of confidence or a sense of not belonging. Or, it could be the belief that you are not 'good enough'. Maybe you feel easily overwhelmed and unable to cope, or you find that you are lonely and can't deal with intimacy. **These issues should not define you,** they are not who you are—they were taught to you or they are what you absorbed along the way!

Let's go back to the metaphor of the tree that is planted in a container that has become too small for it to grow in. Let's assume that each of us has been taught things about ourselves that are not true and that these lessons are in our world view, blocking us from becoming fulfilled and happy. Here's an idea: the tree is one plant but underneath the surface are many roots. These roots are complicated and sometimes grow in tangled ways. When we want to understand ourselves, it may seem that there are too many parts to consider and that it is too difficult a job to get it all sorted out. The truth though, is that we should not let our fears get in the way of our chance to become healthy and whole. If we really examine the roots, we find that although they look messy and confusing they actually support just one plant.

This main system is what needs to be repaired. The tree itself needs to be taken care of. When we talk about personal growth, we are talking about focusing on taking care of one system (that's you)! Personal growth is about bringing your true self out in the healthiest way possible.

When you look over your life you may say, "But I have problems in so many places! I have problems with my girlfriend, parents, kids, boss, and even with myself. How is this just *one* system?" To answer this, it might be helpful to remember that the tree we've been talking about is just one single plant. When you start to work on what's gone wrong for the tree (again, that's you!) *You need to start someplace.*

You can start with one problem but you'll find over time that this one problem connects to all of your other issues. It may seem confusing and difficult at first, but once you get on the right road the process becomes clearer.

Where should self growth begin?

A good place to start the process of self growth is to **choose one basic issue** that is getting in your way. For example, perhaps you want to become kinder to yourself and to other people. We often look at others and judge what we see using terms that are callous, nasty and unforgiving.

People who tend to be judgmental of others tend to be even more critical of themselves

Being critical and judgmental makes it difficult to be happy with yourself and with the important people in your life. In this situation we might have a chronic feeling of dissatisfaction both with ourselves and the world around us.

How can we change this?

We begin by consciously observing our thoughts as we watch the people around us. If we find that we are harsh in our assessments, we tune into our negative thought patterns and strive to willfully replace them with a kinder substitute. The saying goes that we should not judge others until we stand in their shoes. We usually know little about the events that have shaped others. We tend to guess who we think they are, and then assume that this is true. If you are fortunate enough to get to know this person better, chances may be that your shallow first impression was not so accurate after all. Test it! If you find that this is true for you, let's try to see others in a more gentle light, in a compassionate way. It is very difficult to continue to hold onto unrealistic assessments of ourselves and others when we purposefully choose to think in ways that are forgiving, kind and patient.

In my practice, when clients engage in this exercise of awareness and observation, I have noticed that they are often shocked by how much negative judgmental thinking they engage in about other people. I share this insight with my client, and soon after this realization, they begin to notice that they are even tougher on themselves. Once the penny drops, they begin to soften the way they view their surrounding world.

The work of change requires that you first pay attention and catch yourself when you are making overly harsh conclusions about yourself and other people. Self growth happens when you deliberately step in and alter patterns of thought and feelings that you may not have even been aware of before. You make change.

This is where awareness is born.

Make no mistake: change is not easy. Bringing the best of ourselves into our world is one of the most courageous things we can do as adults. There will be days when you won't want to work on yourself or when you feel worried about what all of this change will look like. But it is important to remember that if you commit to this process of self growth and work through the strategies offered in this book step by step, it will lead you towards living a life that truly expresses who you are meant to be in the world. It will free your natural voice and give you the chance to find the challenges that you were always meant to face. As you grow, you will take some missteps and you will probably run into people who will prefer that you stay the way you have always been. The main thing is to keep focused on the goals you have set for yourself and to remember that all of us are on an important life long journey.

Here is a ***summary of the strategy*** to use to be less judgmental:

Step 1	Become aware that you would like to be less judgmental and less critical of yourself and others
Step 2	Consciously observe the people around you at a few different locations (e.g. the park, theatre, shopping mall, coffee shop, your home, work)
Step 3	If you tend to be harsh in your assessment, try to place yourself in their shoes for a moment
Step 4	Substitute the harsh thought with kindness instead
Step 5	Notice how you see the world now
Step 6	Repeat steps one till six whenever the opportunity arises
Step 7	Over time, evaluate the changes it brings about in you

Homework:

- Decide if you want to commit yourself to working on your self growth
- If you do decide in the affirmative, then begin to work through this first strategy step by step
- Focus on this exercise for at least one week to become familiar with how it works for you
- This is the first building block. As you progress, continue to practice this strategy together with those suggested in the upcoming lessons
- Keep practicing until it becomes natural for you to see yourself and others in a kinder light

Lesson 2

Pay Attention

Awareness and Clarity

Now, *practically speaking,* what do we need to do to achieve awareness and clarity?

Awareness brings our intellect back into decision making. When we have our intellect at the ready, it is then there to help us determine a response. Thoughtful, constructive, and intentional conduct is powerful because we are *consciously directing* it.

We are no longer at the mercy of unconscious, predetermined ways of responding.

Awareness allows us to **create a space** to examine our immediate experience. We purposely turn our attention to what is happening, listen to what is being said, see how other people are behaving, then make our own decisions about how to respond. Awareness gives us options.

Once we create this space, we can briefly step back from the situation, and move in a new direction if we choose. When we set out on a new constructive direction, real change happens.

What does it mean to "create a space"? And how do you "step back"?

Creating space happens when you take a step back in your mind, and pull yourself inward so that you can examine what is going on. For example, you find yourself getting into the same old argument with your partner. You notice that this is the beginning of a repeated pattern of behavior between the two of you. So, instead of going ahead and arguing as usual, you pull back for a moment, think about what is happening, and then choose a new path that fits you better. ***You choose*** *how you will engage.*

You change your old patterns.

Whenever we make a space like this **we are automatically drawing appropriate boundaries** between ourselves and other people. Drawing boundaries is a positive step to take because it makes it possible for us to understand how other people's reactions affect us versus how we actually want to behave. Having boundaries means you can call certain things "belonging to me" and other things "belonging to others". Boundaries create a healthy distance between ourselves and other people. The idea is to not to disconnect yourself from others; rather, it is to take responsibility for your own issues and let the other person take care of theirs. Creating a space means we act with intent instead of the automatic reaction that occurs without thought.

For example, I can ask myself: Am I taking responsibility for another person's bad mood? Does this really belong to me? How can I stop myself from repeating my old mistake of being pulled into an emotional whirlwind which really belongs to someone else? Can I let go and let each person deal with their "own issues"?

When we create a space it allows us time to think. We take a moment to quietly ask ourselves: What do *I* want to do? Do I choose, right now, to make a change?" This moment of creating a space removes the emotional component of the issue for a moment and allows us to bring our more objective mind into play. Once we've thought things through, we then can bring emotion back in a managed way.

When we use our intellect, we then have conscious choices available to us and our reactions can be markedly different. Not only do our reactions change, but so do the reactions of others! Consider this: rather than instantly arguing in a defensive and angry manner, **we take a brief moment to think.** We might then calm ourselves and find a new way to discuss a lingering problem. If our intent is to heal, then creating this conscious space instantly interferes with the usual destructive chain of events.

A new path can be taken which benefits everyone!

We can respond to events in our environment constructively as opposed to destructively.

This mental check takes only a split second. Once we're in that quieter, introspective place, we can also analyze the behaviors of those around us. We can question how our behavior affects others and what their behavior tells us about them. We learn from experience and can try to respond more effectively next time.

This brief space of time gives us clarity. We pull ourselves out of old patterns of behavior which have not served us well. We are also allowing ourselves a moment to reflect on what we'd like to do differently. This practical strategy helps us to recognize reactions in ourselves and others that are **emotional triggers**. These are events that spark an instant, unconsciously based response. In recognizing a trigger we can learn to pause, process, and then behave.

After you've practiced the strategy of making a mental check and trying a new approach to an old problem, you can evaluate the process. Take a quick look at what's been learned, discard what was useless and keep what worked. This way you develop a strategy that works specifically for you. New behaviors that are "plugged into" your array of choices will produce increasingly successful, productive behavior over time.

Without awareness this process cannot be initiated.

You might object and say that it is impossible to create this space at the moment that something objectionable is happening. You might say that you are an emotional person and easily swept up into the events around you. However, if you want to make positive changes and have your own behavior more accurately reflect who you are and what you want to be in the world, you need to practice conscious awareness. In doing so, you will be able to understand how other people's conduct affects you and how your own responses contributes to problematic interactions. Seeing those triggers and then responding to them with a behavior which you choose for each circumstance is empowering.

You can do this! Achieving awareness is not complex and it is not something reserved for people who are somehow extraordinary. Awareness is an everyday tool that is available to anyone who wants to be more in control of how they are living.

Since we can't change other people and can only change ourselves, it is our responsibility to make the changes in ourselves that will lead to more positive interactions.

However, in changing our reactions we can *indirectly change* the other person's response to us. For example, when we stop ourselves from automatically engaging in repetitive arguments with our partner, it influences our partner to change his behavior. He can't argue alone, after all! This strategy may also be easily applied to difficult teenagers, socially awkward friends, or even critical parents. The interpersonal dynamic is instantly shifted between you and others when you take the conscious step to take possession of what is yours and what is not.

Awareness puts you in touch with yourself and others. It is enlivening, and not usually selfish or self-focused. Awareness prepares you to make real and enduring connections with the world to achieve your greatest dreams. Awareness translates into clarity, which then provides the light on your path forward.

Clarity is when we can see ourselves clearly without the interference of convoluted, confused, unhelpful thinking.

With clarity, we can see our direction ahead of us as if the sun were brightly shining overhead. To live a meaningful life, we must have vision. Clarity allows us to place our steps where we want them to be. When we walk with intent and are no longer slaves to unconscious processes, we are the master of ourselves and our reactions. Clarity makes it possible for us to listen more accurately to our inner voice.

What is this inner voice?

The inner voice is that quiet place within us, that place of *knowing*. This is the place where we connect spiritually to the universe. We should not confuse our inner voice with our ego. The inner voice is not self centered or constantly demanding attention. The inner voice is not actually our conscience, but is connected to it.

The inner voice is who we genuinely are, how we truly want to behave, and what we really feel and believe.

Our inner voice is our pure self, uncomplicated and unburdened by the demands of others and the negativity that is often found in our environment. Clarity permits us to perceive the messages of the inner voice and then to act on them. When we act on these messages, we are behaving in ways that are in tune with our natural selves. These natural selves are how we were when we came into the world but which are often damaged or hidden by events in our childhood. Clarity opens a window to our higher selves, and it is when we respond faithfully to this healthy self that we are most likely to feel happiness.

Everyone has a unique job to do in the world. With awareness, we can act to refine our genuine personality and improve on all levels: personally, within our families, within our community, and in the universe as well. We automatically are significant by virtue of our being here, but we can get stuck acting in ways which deflect us from our purpose. You are one person among many others, but you are utterly unique.

You can think of your life holistically, taking in spiritual, emotional, and intellectual parts of yourself as you do so. Life flows easily when we accept and use all of ourselves to express who we are in the world. When we are faced with difficult circumstances, we can go back to this idea of life as a flowing sea with currents and streams in it, which vary and change over time. We all know that we have good days and bad. When we anticipate the ebb and flow of life, the difficult times can be so much easier!

This meditation is a useful tool to help you focus:

Life is like a wave.
It swells forth and settles back
Up and down we go
Some days are easier
Others more difficult
Yet over time
Our lives will flow
Like a meandering stream
Drifting here and there sometimes
Other times
Surging strong and sure

Here is a ***summary of the strategy*** to achieve awareness:

Step 1	Become aware that you are beginning to have a negative reaction to something (an emotional trigger)
Step 2	Mentally step back and create a space to think about what is really going on
Step 3	Separate what belongs to you and what belongs to the other person
Step 4	Set out the possible response choices before you
Step 5	Choose a higher level response and act on it
Step 6	Notice the others person's reaction
Step 7	Discard what didn't work and build on what was successful to use in the future
Step 8	Take time to evaluate the whole process. Ask yourself: What have I learned?

Homework:

- Use the awareness strategy above as a guide to build your self awareness

Lesson 3

Take a Belly Breath

The Gift of Breath

Sit back for a moment and think about the act of breathing. Allow yourself, just now, to feel your breath coming in and going out of your body. You'll notice that the soft air comes in through your nose and mouth, fills your chest and then you exhale again.

Let's try…

Breathe in

Breathe out

Breathe in

Breathe out

Breathe in

Breathe out.

What do you notice?

Most of us don't give any thought to this amazing foundational part of our lives. So, what about **breathing with intent**?

Breathing is a vital gift which keeps us alive. It is involuntary and universal. All of us in the human community and all of the living creatures beyond it, breathe. We don't intend to breathe and because of that we take it for granted unless something happens to interfere with our natural ability to inhale and exhale. But breathing is actually a gift that confers life. Without breath we are almost instantly thrown into a state of unconsciousness.

If we breathe with intent, could we become ***more aware****?*

Yes! **Belly breathing** brings direct awareness to us in a powerful and yet simple way. This technique allows us to breathe with consciousness and provides a resting space between us and our more harmful emotional states. Belly breathing (which could also be called *intentional breathing*) is a mindful response that creates a "space" in which we can consider the many choices available to us before we react. Conscious control over our reactions is so important, since whenever we bring our intellects to bear we are bringing awareness into our lives and we are also choosing how we will behave.

Choice making is liberating!

How do we do belly breathing? Try this: sit somewhere comfortable and relax your shoulders. Create a quiet, safe place in your mind by imagining a room or a place outdoors that is peaceful and easy to be in. Take your time. Then, once you feel relaxed, place the tip of your tongue behind your upper teeth. This regulates the flow of air into your body. Take a long, slow breath in, noticing how this breath expands your abdomen. Under ordinary circumstances, we breathe more shallowly, expanding only our upper lungs. When you slowly, mindfully breathe, it almost feels as if you are sidestepping your lungs. The breath goes directly to your belly. The chest then expands as well, as this deep breath enters the remaining space above. Once you have filled your lungs, release the entire breath evenly.

If you get dizzy, remind yourself that you are intending to breathe deeply into your belly. Take slow breaths and be sure to exhale completely before starting again.

What do you accomplish when you use the belly breathing technique?

When you breathe like this, you bring a considerably greater amount of cleansing air into your body. Because you have taken a deeper, fuller breath, essentially massaging nearby organs, you produce a relaxing effect in the body. Your greater exhalation has also removed much more toxins or pollutants from your system, making it easier for your brain to work freely. You have also mindfully chosen to slow yourself down, bring yourself to a greater level of serenity, and taken the time to be good to yourself.

If we agree that breathing is a gift that makes life possible, then we can take a step further and say that breathing mindfully can make us feel more powerful in our lives. Whenever we do something, *with intent,* even something very basic like breathing, we are taking control of our actions.

If, for example, someone says or does something which makes us feel angry, we can choose to react with anger, hostility and even aggression. It may be that as children we learned to imitate other peoples' responses in heated circumstances because we watched adults, who were our role models, behave angrily or in ways that were out of control.

We may have been taught that if we are angry, it is right and necessary to immediately respond with aggressive reactions.

The problem with this lesson is obvious. If we respond angrily to every provocation, we are likely to end up with even more trouble on our hands! Problems are not resolved, and it is also destructive for the people around us. When we hurt others it is very difficult to feel good about ourselves.

We may have been told that when we get angry it is good to let it all out, to get it out of your system.

We should question this assumption.

More often than not, we feel worse when anger has free reign.

In order to break into this cycle, it is useful to become more measured in our responses. The first step in doing this is to take a step back and become self-aware. Breathing mindfully is one of the most basic tools that we can use to open ourselves up to self-awareness.

Angry reactions can be like a reflex. That, is, we can feel and act angrily without thinking about it. *When an angry response is reflexive, like a knee jerk response to a tap on the knee, then it is time to understand our anger better and to gain control of it.*

Since breathing is with us constantly, we can use belly breathing whenever we are in a situation that could provoke destructive emotional reactions. Similarly, we can use this simple technique when we are anxious, overwhelmed, or overexcited. For example, we might notice when we're at the dentist's office, that we are becoming anxious. Our palms are sweating, we feel like pacing, and we are instantly aggravated by ringing telephones or by the sounds of the dentist's equipment in the background. Using belly breathing in this situation instantly provides relief.

How does that happen?

Belly breathing is aware breathing. As we have already seen, it focuses the mind, brings purifying, cleansing air into our whole system, and discharges greater volumes of irritants and pollutants. But belly breathing accomplishes more than that. When we stop our childish or immature reactions and instead select new behaviors which are more fitting for us, we are in charge of ourselves. By taking control over these negative behaviors and substituting them with healthy and controlled reactions, we are instantly freed to make more insightful choices. We become empowered. You could say that this gives us the opportunity to begin the process of enlightened living.

Belly breathing, like breath itself, is a gift. Unlike regular breathing, it is not natural to us. We have to learn how to do it. Still, the little time that it takes to learn is well worth the effort! Beyond learning how to belly breathe, we need to practice it, the way you might practice any new skill. Once you've learned how to do it and when to use it, you can take it anywhere and use it under any stressful circumstances. Remember: this skill is only one of many that are available to you, and with practice it will become part of your everyday life!

One of the beauties of this technique is that it is free.

Belly breathing is always there for you, it is not time consuming, and it doesn't require extraordinary effort on your part. You don't need to go to any gym or exercise class to use it. You just need to mindfully turn it on!

When you belly breathe, you should notice that you feel brighter and more alert. This is because more oxygen and deeper breathing us feel healthier and happier. When the cells of the body are deprived of oxygen they cannot function to their greatest extent. This is why shallow breathing often makes people feel panicky, unwell and even faint.

This relaxed, enhanced breathing gives us time to slow down a bit.

You can practice this technique anytime. You can take it wherever you go. You can even try this when you are shopping or driving. Once you have mastered the technique, use it when you notice that you are feeling upset or when you are in a situation that provokes anxiety or anger. Going to a doctor's office, to the dentist, to the airport or into a courthouse are all good examples of places where this technique should be applied. Some people like to use belly breathing when they are in school before a test or when they are going to a job interview or meeting someone new. Whenever you are in circumstances in which you notice you are feeling less relaxed, you should also be able to notice that you are breathing more shallowly. It is at that point that you should use belly breathing.

It should always work for you!

Here is the ***summary of the belly breathing*** exercise:

Step 1	Sit comfortably and relax your shoulders. Prepare yourself to breathe with awareness
Step 2	Imagine a place of beauty, serenity and safety
Step 3	Spread the tip of your tongue behind your upper teeth
Step 4	Take a long, slow controlled breath into your belly
Step 5	Feel your abdomen expand. Hold your breath for a few seconds
Step 6	Slowly exhale and release your breath
Step 7	Repeat until you feel relaxed and clear headed
Step 8	Evaluate the entire process. Use whenever needed for relaxation and clarity

Homework

- Think of a place of beauty, serenity, and safety. Use this image when you practice your belly breathing
- Close your eyes and take your time. Once you have a clear picture of this spot, anchor it in your mind so that you can access it easily
- Use your breath to manage anxiety, angry outbursts, or other negative knee-jerk responses

Lesson 4

Live Now!

Past, Present and Future

We all have a past, present, and future. We don't always understand how these three instances of time work together. Unfortunately, we often keep our past too close to us.

Doing so shadows our future, and prevents us from experiencing the present.

Past events in your life are now out of your reach. You have lived it, and it is gone. We cannot go back in time. As time moves forward, events in our past move farther and farther back into our history.

Time can be compared to a flowing river. If you were to drop a leaf on the surface of the water while you are standing on the bank, you could watch the leaf move past you, eventually disappearing beyond your view.

Your past cannot be changed, but we can learn to perceive it differently in the present.

This is called **reframing**.

Most of us have a set of beliefs which are central to the way in which we understand the world. We have had these beliefs for so long, and refer to them often enough that we don't even notice them anymore and just assume that they are true. These beliefs, however, can get in our way and prevent us from being able to see what is going on around us in a clear way. For example, you might believe that everything you do is bound to fail. Because you feel this way you will be less likely to get out there and try new things. Your belief that you will fail *stops you* from taking calculated risks.

Even if this risk is likely to succeed, you won't attempt it simply because this core belief of yours gets in the way. What if you open your mind to the possibility that you are wrong? What if this core belief is similar to an old habit that you can change?

When you reframe, you give yourself the opportunity to gain perspective and to look again at an old story in a new, hopeful way. You change the parameters and rules that you've been functioning under and challenge outdated assumptions. You give yourself the chance to succeed!

Humans are a very complicated species. We are faced with complex issues almost from the moment we first come into this world. What if *every one of us is meant to discover our own area of challenge* and use this knowledge to benefit ourselves and the world around us?

By improving our areas of challenge, we can produce positive outcomes and refine the world.

We can take the suffering that we've experienced in the past, and put it into context if we think about things in this way.

We can reframe.

So what happens if we don't *want* to work on a given challenge?

What if, instead of looking at things from a fresh perspective, we hold on to the anger and pain that comes with our negative core beliefs? Chances are that someone who holds on to pain will remain haunted or controlled by the events which produced the pain. Holding on to past negativity can devastate a life, distort it, and make it nearly impossible to live happily.

With this awareness, we are able to see painful past events as important, without letting them hold us hostage. We have used reframing to clarify our perspective and make new decisions. Holding on to past pain without using it as a means to learn about ourselves is self-defeating.

It's important that we look honestly at the events that mould us. It is also essential that we use our intellect to put what happened to us into context. In Lesson One of *Lessons from a Life Coach* we discussed how childhood experiences can have profound and lasting effects on how we see ourselves and others later on in life.

As mentioned previously, we understand that to some degree we are all products of our childhood experiences. If we choose, we can look back and discern *now* what we couldn't understand then. We can notice where our family patterns worked for us or against us.

How? We can use our newfound awareness to review how we relate to other people presently, and how our own behavior keeps us stuck.

We can challenge the childhood assumptions that we have carried with us into our young adult and mature years. Then, we can either replay these old patterns or rather; we can find more purposeful, positive ways to relate to others.

Imagine that you have been placed into your particular family for a reason.

By this we mean that it is not a roll of the dice that leads us to be born into a particular family; rather, we are put there for a specific purpose. This purpose may not be clear to us at a young age but it can certainly become clear to us as we mature.

Consider this idea: The family that we were born into provides us with the dynamics that set us up for a particular purpose and it is within our family dynamic that our most basic challenges take shape.

Now let's challenge those childhood assumptions by reframing the untrue core beliefs. This puts into place a healthy system that we build consciously for ourselves. For example, we might hold on to a core belief such as:

"There is something wrong with me!"

"I'm no good."

"I don't belong."

"It's all my fault."

"I don't deserve to be happy."

"I should be punished."

"I'm a victim."

"I'm entitled."

All of these core beliefs keep us shackled to damaging self defeating behaviors. What we were given as rules or truths from our particular family dynamic are not supposed to hold us as prisoners to our past. This is where our life's work must be done— it is where our distinct and unique challenges are. When those core beliefs do keep us stuck, they play out in our present as social awkwardness, anxiety, feelings of powerlessness or self-centeredness, etc. All of these outcomes are negative and interfere with our ability to be joyful in the present and future.

When we are stuck we believe that we have few choices. Under these circumstances, we will tend to make the same mistakes over and over again and find it very difficult to learn from our past experience.

The present is with us now.

The present is where we live, breathe, and interact. It is also where we have the greatest power to consciously change our circumstances. While our past cannot be altered, we can directly affect our present as it is happening. Now, as adults, we have the option to choose to select either old negative behaviors or new, healthier ways of interacting.

We cannot change our past, but when we make healthy choices in the present, we can anticipate a happier future for ourselves.

The purpose of understanding past, present, and future is to work toward freeing ourselves and making sure we are no longer stuck within the confines of negative thinking. Even though the past cannot be changed it can become a powerful tool in our empowerment!

When we use our past to see things differently, we are immediately open to new ideas. These new ideas are likely to be more mature, rational, and healthy than the ideas we previously had.

Children might not be able to gain insight about their circumstances but now as adults, we can!

In order to make the idea of core beliefs easier to understand and work with, here is a short vignette for you to review:

> Marcy grew up with a narcissistic mother whose only interest was herself. Marcy tried constantly to please her mother and was careful not to make her angry. Marcy's father gave in to her mother's every whim and rarely gave Marcy any of his time or attention. As a result, Marcy grew up with a core belief that *she didn't matter.* She had almost no parental guidance and felt overwhelmed throughout her childhood and adolescence. She had difficulty making decisions. Even though she needed others' approval, she developed a distrust of people and therefore had no true support system and few resources to rely on. When she grew into a young adult, Marcy often ignored her own needs and feelings and allowed other people to use her. She often felt sad, isolated, and alone even when surrounded by people. She had low self esteem and little confidence in her abilities. Her relationships were shallow and unrewarding and she didn't understand why she always felt unloved and ignored by other

people. Finally, when the sadness began to darken, Marcy decided to seek help. Over time, she realized that her relationships were one-sided and unrewarding. Once she connected her present day problems with how she was treated as a child, she worked harder on feeling good about herself and less dependent on the approval of others. Marcy knew that she had to overcome her lack of trust in people. She noticed when people were supportive and kind then chose to surround herself with these genuinely caring friends. She focused on developing relationships that were wholesome by clearly asking for what she needed and by setting limits when she felt that other people were taking advantage of her. She became more open and giving of herself to the people she could trust. Over time, and with practice, she began to feel empowered and happier. She learned to recognize the feelings that would sometimes surface as belonging to her untrue *'I do not matter'* core belief. As she became more aware and learned to associate this childhood belief in her present world, she used strategies (like the ones outlined above) to avoid falling into old negative patterns of feeling negatively about herself.

Here is a ***summary of the strategy*** to reframe your untrue core beliefs:

Step 1	Become aware that you are currently stuck in a particular place in your life
Step 2	Ask yourself if this particular sensation of being 'stuck' feels familiar
Step 3	Try to associate being 'stuck' with a learned childhood *untrue core belief*
Step 4	Challenge this childhood assumption
Step 5	Clarify for yourself in *words* or *writing* what this insight teaches you
Step 6	With this new clarity, try to reframe your *untrue core belief*
Step 7	Notice how negative past experience impacts your present state of mind
Step 8	Evaluate what you have learned. Use this technique to learn more about the other *untrue core beliefs* which prevent your personal growth and happiness

Homework

- Take a moment to think about the idea of whether you believe past experience impacts your present-day perspective on life

Lesson 5

Stop the Head Chatter

Focus!

"The human condition is one of struggle against unwanted thoughts bombarding us at every moment." (*Methuselah*, 2011).

Thought is a constant for us as humans. From the moment you wake up in the morning until you fall asleep at night thoughts are bombarding us. The fascinating thing about this is that most of us are largely unaware of all these thoughts. When asked what we're thinking about, most of the time the majority of us might reply "nothing". But this is not true!

Our minds are constantly active as we process everything around us, filter information, sift through memories, create new ideas, make connections, and plan actions.

It may be for our benefit that we are mainly unaware of all of these thoughts, because if we were able to hear all of them on a conscious level we would be so overwhelmed that we wouldn't be able to function much at all! The problem is that sometimes these thoughts are anxiety producing and we, being unaware of them, find ourselves feeling anxious and upset without knowing why.

Our thoughts come in and out of our minds extremely quickly. In fact, there is a constant background 'buzz' of thoughts so that we often can't differentiate between them or silence them.

For some people the anxiety or uneasiness that they feel is due to negative thoughts which may be troubling and repetitive. These thoughts are unproductive and even detrimental to us. At times, people can feel overwhelmed by the anxiety that this hectic thinking creates. In order to protect ourselves against this rising tide of anxiety, we may try to separate ourselves from these thoughts, but this only leads to more trouble.

When we are alienated or separated from our thinking, it is easy to believe that we are no longer in control of our thoughts. We might even begin to believe that there is something wrong with us.

Usually, there isn't anything seriously wrong with us at all !

When we find ourselves in this peculiar disconnected state we can say that we are stuck in a situation that can be called head chatter.

What is head chatter? As you might have guessed from the name, the term "head chatter" could best be described as a jumble of ideas and thoughts that seem to have free rein to run around in our heads unchecked. In this situation, it's as if we are standing on a tennis court surrounded by people batting hundreds of balls past us, over our heads, hitting us occasionally. It's chaotic!

We can take control of what happens in our minds and dramatically reduce our anxiety. Beyond this, we may also become more focused and empowered, and have the tools to better deal with the complexities of our lives in a productive way.

How do we go about reducing head chatter?

First, assume that you have the ability to control your thoughts. You don't have to be passive! The fact that there is such a large amount of activity going on does not mean you must simply stand by helplessly. However, controlling your thinking and being in touch with it does mean that discipline, focus, and consistency are necessary.

Let's start this process of reducing chatter to a manageable level. Select a phrase that is meaningful, positive, and inspirational to you. You may find this phrase in a book, in a poem, on a sign, in the Bible, in the lyrics of a song, in nature, or anywhere you like. Your inspirational phrase should not be longer than five to seven words.

Learn it by heart so you can use it immediately whenever you need it.

Now, let's go through the strategy to gain awareness in order to stop head chatter and the anxiety which often accompanies it:

1. Be aware that head chatter exists and that it interferes with your concentration. This is true for everyone. *Having awareness is the necessary first step to making any change.*

2. Remind yourself that the mind never rests. However, it can hold only one thought at a time. Although thoughts are arriving so fast to your brain that your head seems to buzz with them, the truth is that only one idea can be present in your mind at any one moment.

3. Recall the inspirational phrase that you memorized for this exact moment. This action transfers away the energy that had been used for "chatter" toward a subject of your own conscious choosing. This phrase is a corrective action, helping you to focus and slow down, stopping the head chatter for a moment.

4. You may use visualization with your phrase to increase its impact. Visualization is a tool that helps you stay with clarified thinking. You can use the belly breathing strategy to help you focus and to maintain calm as well.

5. Give your inspirational phrase your full attention. Focus. Conscious awareness and purposeful thinking is the opposite of head chatter and the two cannot exist at once. At this moment, you are now focused and in control of your thoughts!

6. Now, allow the phrase to be set aside and do a quick check. Compare the clarity you feel now with the chaos that came before.

7. Evaluate how this tool has helped you.

Once you have used the same phrase for a while, you will probably find that it no longer has the same focusing effect it used to. This is because your phrase, as it comes more easily to you, requires you to use less intellectual energy to focus on it. This intellectual energy is necessary to divert your attention away from head chatter. It's important that you change your phrase as needed so that you will continue to benefit from this strategy.

In time, and with practice, this strategy will empower you to reduce head chatter to a manageable level.

Not all head chatter is unconscious or overwhelming. Sometimes we find ourselves aware of thoughts that seems out of our control, repetitive, and exhausting. This is called "hamsterwheeling".

"Hamsterwheeling" is like the little brother of head chatter.

The term hamsterwheeling refers to the tendency of becoming stuck in a repeated pattern of thinking that one can't seem to break out of.

Like a hamster in an exercise wheel, we get started in a particular pattern of thoughts. We run and run and run without ever getting anywhere! When you hamsterwheel, you are stuck. You are not achieving change and you are not making decisions. Instead, you are using up valuable energy on repetitive thought patterns that are not helping you.

The difference between head chatter and hamsterwheeling is that people may quickly notice when they are getting into that hamster wheel. You can practice the same strategy with hamsterwheeling as you will use for head chatter. Interfering with this noisy background and being able to focus more easily is extremely empowering!

Aside from the fact that distraction and anxiety are uncomfortable, our potential for happiness and empowerment are blocked if we are stuck running in circles. Our goal is to have a life in which we live out our best self and achieve the goals and dreams that we hope for.

Once head chatter is diminished, you will find that your thinking is more articulate and clear. Your decision making skills and behavior are more controlled and purposeful.

We are all in this world for a purpose that is unique to each individual.

If you are stuck in a never ending loop it's unlikely that you'll be able to strike out on your true life's path.

Imagine that we are all existing on a three dimensional plane that is shaped like a spring or a helix. The spring has loops that connect to one another, advancing upwards. As you proceed from one stage to the next higher one, you are continuously refining who you are and what you are capable of. You are always evolving closer and closer to fulfilling your individual promise as a human being.

Once you have dealt effectively with head chatter and its little brother, hamsterwheeling, you can leap out of the monotonous circle and move forwards into the first spiral of this spring.

You become aligned with your inner world and live genuinely.

Why is this beneficial?

Each of us is like a gem with many facets. In our earliest days we are unpolished and to the casual observer, not particularly clear. When we are held back by old issues and intrusions such as head chatter, our uniqueness, beauty, and clarity of vision cannot be revealed. As we work on ourselves, it's as if we are polishing each facet, revealing more and more of who we truly are and what we were put in the world to do. We begin to shine!

Here is a ***summary of the strategy*** to alleviate head chatter:

Step 1	Become aware that you are experiencing head chatter
Step 2	Remind yourself that the mind can hold only one thought at a time
Step 3	Consciously recall the inspirational phrase you have memorized
Step 4	Use the visualization technique to focus your attention
Step 5	Give the inspirational phrase your full concentration
Step 6	Now relax and ask yourself: "Am I more centered? More focused?"
Step 7	Repeat the exercise as often as you need
Step 8	Evaluate by comparing your present mental state to before you began

Homework

- Select an inspirational phrase
- Memorize the phrase
- Use the phrase as described in the strategy above

Lesson 6

Choose Well

Making Healthy Choices

We are making choices all the time. Many of our choices are unconscious or automatic. **Unconscious choices** can be quite simple (like automatically starting the coffee maker in the morning) or more complicated (like forgetting to get in touch with an old friend on her birthday) but they are all bound together by the fact that we don't give them conscious thought or planning, *they just seem to happen.*

Conscious choices can also be quite simple or they may have dramatic effects. For example, we have simple choices like whether we'll turn left or right as we exit a building, if we'll go to the gym today or skip it, or whether we'll buy that new shirt or leave it on the shelf. Similarly, conscious choices may be more complex, such as, if we'll take a certain job, when we'll call the doctor about a recurring pain, or if we'll continue in a relationship.

The idea of healthy choice making is to **actively select** what our course of action will be. This applies to the short, medium, and long term goals that we set for ourselves. Learning to make healthy decisions is extremely important.

We are often not taught the skills of how to make healthy choices.

As young people we learn to make decisions based on the direction our parents think is right for us. Alternatively, we might take the quickest and simplest option offered to us without giving the consequences much thought. The result of unexamined choice making could be that when we are adults we rush ourselves through decisions, depriving ourselves of the chance to think things through.

Under these hurried circumstances, we miss out on the opportunity to learn about ourselves and what it is that we truly need to be contributing to the world.

Healthy choice making takes into account how other people are affected by our decisions.

Our choices make us who we are, and actualize us as people.

If we continue to make choices which take us in the wrong direction, it's as if we are salmon heading up the wrong stream. When we listen to ourselves and make decisions that are right for us, we are in tune with our inner voice and thus are able to express our unique selves in the world.

Many people make the mistake of being overly influenced by their emotions when making decisions. Although emotions are an important part of choice, they are subjective. At the emotional level, we are more likely to make choices based on "what's good for me" rather than "what is good". That is why our intellect must be **very** involved in the process as well.

The intellect is more objective by nature.

In the following pages you will find a strategy that brings both intellect and conscious awareness into choice-making. You can apply this strategy to both simple and complex problems. Since practice is the key to becoming familiar with this exercise, I suggest that you follow the steps to making healthy choices until the process becomes second nature to you.

The goal is to fully think things through *before* we act.

Here is a strategy for healthy choice-making:

1. Become aware that you are being presented with a choice (this means allowing yourself to see that you can pick between at least two possible outcomes). Sit back for a moment and think over your situation and then review your options. You may have thought that you had to pick one way of doing things. You may be used to doing this particular thing in a certain way and never thought of approaching it from a different angle. Perhaps your group of friends takes a particular approach to this choice. Maybe now you'd like to try something new. Or you may need a solution which is more effective, pleasing, or simply easier. **Now you know you have the possibility of choice**.

2. With an open mind, consider the many options available to you. Since you are now "thinking outside the box", you can see that there are new possibilities for action (this may mean taking no action at all!). Dream up all the choices, including the most bizarre ones. *You aren't taking any action yet, so all possibilities are available to you.*

3. From all of your possible options, pick a few which appeal to you most. You have now reduced the number of choices you have to mull over. Obviously some choices are better than others. You are your own person with your own individual style. Your mom and dad might have always done things in one way but you are yourself. In what way do *you* want to do things? The choices you select as most appealing probably reflect who you are. Now begin to look at which options are practical and which are unlikely to work at all. Abandon the impractical choices. At this point you should have reduced the serious choices in front of you to three or four.

4. Thoroughly research the few options you have selected. This is the time consuming part. Get on to the internet, make a few phone calls, talk to people, do whatever you can to gather necessary information about your options. For example, if you're thinking about moving to a new apartment and you know which neighborhoods appeal to you most, do some research on rental prices, on locations of shops, bus stops, and other neighborhood features that will be important to you. Look at time lines, financial implications, travel distances to work, and convenience factors.

5. Analyze the data you have gathered. To analyze data you don't have to be a scientist! You can simply write a list of pros and cons. Be honest with yourself as you write. When making your decision consider how your choice could affect the significant people in your life. You should also be thinking about what you want to have in your next job that you don't have now and whether your goals are doable and likely to succeed.

6. This is the opportune time to bring your emotions into play. Up till now, we have been handling this choice in a fairly intellectual manner. We might want to ask ourselves questions like: How do I feel about this? How does it affect the people I care about? Will I be happy with this? Can I see myself doing this? Does this fit who I am becoming? Can I anticipate some of the future ramifications? Will this have a positive affect in the world?

7. Make your decision. Design a step by step plan and commit to it.

8. Put your plan into action — actualize your choice!

9. Give the choice time to mature, while observing the process as it unfolds.

10. Now evaluate how the process is unfolding. Keep checking to confirm if the decision is working. Are your goals being met? If you can answer yes to this question, well done! If not, allow yourself to re-evaluate.

If your initial choice does not work out as you had planned, allow yourself to re-think your choice, make essential changes, and re-commit to your adjusted plan. It isn't a sign of weakness or defeat to re-think your strategy! In fact, making informed adjustments predicts a more successful outcome. Think about what you know from your history lessons. Presidents, kings, and generals changed their decisions as new issues, options, and problems became evident and so can you!

Your goals may stay the same but your ways of achieving those goals can be modified as time goes on. Leave your options open. Although you've made a commitment, you are always free to re-think your decision and add to it or alter it to better suit you. Have the confidence in yourself to adjust to a changing world!

Sometimes, when we are done wrestling with the various options and finally make a decision, it may feel so right – it's as if a bell rings and resonates with every fibre of your being. There is nothing left to discuss.

The path ahead becomes crystal clear. That's when you know you have made the right choice.

It's good to remember that achieving certain goals can take years to accomplish. This may sound daunting *but the truth is that a life marked by awareness is a continuing process. The journey demands consciousness and with that, healthy choices.* You will need to develop both flexibility and the ability to tough things out.

Here is a scenario to illustrate the technique of healthy conscious choice making:

> Kim has always loved horses and wants to ride competitively. She is married to Brad, has three young children and lives in a large city. She works full time as a successful photographer but she is dissatisfied with her life. Kim takes care of the children in the afternoons and she also does all of the housework. She loves her husband and home and she knows her children are happy in their schools. But her dream is to spend her days in a stable, working with horses. The stable she likes best is outside the city, more than an hour away. Brad is unwilling to move out of the city because his extended family lives close by and he feels that if Kim leaves her job they will struggle financially. They can't live on just one salary. Kim isn't sure what to do. She feels like she has to choose between her marriage, her family, and the possibility of fulfilling her dreams.
>
> The likelihood of Kim's success (should she choose to go immediately with her dream) is uncertain. She loves her husband and children but her desire to work with horses puts everyone else's happiness in jeopardy. How can she have what she dreams of without losing so much of what she values? **Since making a healthy choice must be realistic and achievable**, it appears that this is a situation in which Kim will not be able to achieve what she wants and needs without building in some balance to her choice. She cannot work with horses full time at this moment.

However, if we look closer, we can see that while Kim can't move out of the city and devote herself entirely to her dream now, she can certainly find ways to put part of her dream into action. She can actualize her dream by figuring out if she can change her work schedule so that she can spend part of her time working in the closest available stables.

She can talk to Brad about whether he can be more flexible with his schedule and take over some of the child care duties that she has shouldered on her own up until now. She can consider all of her choices —she need not choose between her marriage and her dreams. She should remind herself that her happiness may be eluding her for other reasons. She may need to explore other aspects of her life more deeply. Kim decides, with Brad's agreement, to work part time in photography and part time at the closest stables. He agrees to adjust his schedule to be with the children more often, and they hire cleaning help once a week. They also decide they will re-evaluate these choices in six months. Kim is happier and feels closer to Brad now. Brad is content because what is important to him has been honored. Kim and Brad have realized that their relationship does better when they consider the needs of their partner as well as their own. Their relationship has improved dramatically because they are communicating openly and therefore understand each other better.

You can see from this scenario that if an initial choice isn't realistic, goals may be adjusted. Exploring options and experimenting with choices is positive. This promotes self-awareness and self-esteem. Over time, a dream may be expanded. For example, in Kim's case, she might be able to work full time with horses when the children grow older and more independent, and when the family is more financially stable.

When we feel on track with our decisions, we are empowered. What does it mean to be on track? It is when we are going in a direction that suits us and our goals, and takes us where we hope to go. When we are on track we are in sync with our inner voice.

We no longer feel stuck and uncomfortable in our lives. We are able to approach the challenges we face with courage because our path to achieving our goals is clarified.

The part of ourselves that reflects most clearly who we are and who we want to become is being expressed.

When we make a healthy choice, it becomes a reflection of our inner world, our genuine selves. When we engage that self we are stronger and we can chart our course in a planned, calm, healthy way that benefits the whole universe.

Here is the ***summary of the strategy*** for making healthy choices:

Step 1	Become aware that you are being presented with a choice
Step 2	Be creative and open to all of your possible options. Mull them over
Step 3	Select a few options that appeal to you. Abandon the unworkable ideas
Step 4	Thoroughly research the few selected options
Step 5	Analyze the data you have gathered.
Step 6	Bring your emotions into play. Ask yourself how you feel about your choices
Step 7	Make an informed decision
Step 8	Design a plan of action and commit to it
Step 9	Observe how the plan is unfolding, allowing a reasonable time for it to mature
Step 10	Evaluate the process and make changes to the plan if necessary

Homework

- Think about some of the decisions facing you now
- Select one decision to practice the strategy for making healthy choices
- Use the steps of this strategy as a guideline to make your decision
- Compare this process to how you made your choices in the past
- Ask yourself which model for decision-making works best for you

Lesson 7

Fly Free

Letting Go

Letting go is difficult for many people. We are often taught that we can't be quitters, we must have our day in court, it's not our fault, we must have the last word, **we are always right!** It is these lessons which often hold us back and keep us stuck in old patterns that don't benefit us. Letting go isn't simply about ending our anger, resentment, pain and guilt. When we stop blaming other people for wronging us we can permit ourselves to put down our weapons and ***move on***.

Letting go is not weakness or cowardice.

Why is letting go so important in the creation and maintenance of a healthy, joyful life?

It is often said that when we let go, we free ourselves.

When we choose not to remain under the power of intense emotions (for example, pointless anger), we are taking charge and mindfully selecting how we want to respond to the world around us. Letting go is a powerful choice that liberates the self and allows for new directions. It is a sign of strength to make conscious healthy choices especially when we have done the opposite in the past and reacted without much thought! When you use your energy for choice making instead of pointless arguing you may find that you can reframe old disagreements and start afresh.

Letting go is the way toward flowing through life rather than fighting through it! Flowing with the tide sets us in tune with nature. We fully utilize our energy for the good. We become efficient and effective.

How do we get to efficiency and effectiveness?

This is often very difficult for many people because we tend to set very high, unrealistic goals for ourselves. While it's good to have high standards and work diligently towards our dreams, it is a problem when we demand things of ourselves that aren't realistically achievable.

If we look at our goals do we see ourselves moving steadily through the process from beginning to end in a step-by-step fashion or are we trying, instead, to leap ahead right from A to Z? Or maybe we aren't suited for the goals that we've set for ourselves because we are striving to mimic the apparent successes of other people. We want to be them!

Instead of setting unrealistic goals we need to honor ourselves and our own unique mission.

We may refuse to believe that our goals will take us months or years to reach. We put much pressure on ourselves and then we are disappointed when we don't succeed. We become impatient with the process and try to rush ourselves even though the timing isn't right. This pressure and frustration which we direct against ourselves can start a vicious cycle of disappointment and disbelief in our ability to achieve any goals at all.

What if you let go of unreachable goals and demands? What if instead, you make a fair appraisal of your abilities, needs, beliefs and goals? You can still decide to hold on to your original goals or you might change one or more of them, but in either case you will let go of demands that cannot be met while looking forward to achieving meaningful and productive outcomes. Once you have achieved the first step you can launch yourself from there to a higher level, always keeping in mind that this is a process which must take time to complete. By letting go of what is unrealistic, you are treating yourself fairly and with kindness while still remaining motivated to being creative and effective. You stop punishing yourself pointlessly and look forward, allowing yourself to move through the necessary steps to achieve your dreams.

On the other hand, when we have done all that we can do and put our full effort into our plans, then it is time to let go and give the results over to the universe. Once you have put in all the effort that you possibly can and you are satisfied with your contribution, keep in mind that larger forces outside yourself will be there to pick up the process and help move it along as well.

Letting go and moving forward are also vital to relationships. Imagine a close relationship such as a partnership or a marriage. In any marriage there are misunderstandings and arguments. This is because we marry someone who is not similar to us in every way, and so there are going to be many differences which can create high levels of friction. We should learn from each argument and try to avoid replaying old patterns that don't resolve core issues. Letting go of old useless patterns allows us to better respond to what we wish to communicate and to hear the wants and needs of the other person.

Here is another way to look at what letting go can mean: Imagine that you have a skin infection known as a boil. Boils are very painful because the skin is being stretched and below the surface of the skin there is an infection. The pain can be very great because of the stress that is placed on delicate tissue. You go to the doctor and she lances the boil for you, opening up the skin and draining the infection away. You might have thought that lancing would be intolerably painful but actually, the effect of the lancing is to instantly relieve the pain you were suffering from. The infection drains rapidly away and the skin is returned to its previous state. You are now healthy and pain free.

Holding on to pain and refusing to move on is like having an untreated boil. By gaining insight, making changes, working on your challenges and forgiving, you are effectively lancing that infection. Letting go is liberating because all of the energy that you used to put into your old anger, pain, fear and anxiety is now freed to be used for constructive endeavors instead.

Think of all the energy you can regain for what you've always wanted to accomplish!

Sometimes, of course, we may work towards something and not be successful. If you see that your work is not leading you to achieve what you had hoped for then it is wise to re-think your strategy and to consider letting it go completely. Your moment may just not be now.

Timing matters.

If changing your direction is necessary, then that may be part of our unique challenge as well.

In doing this, we become kinder to ourselves, more open to our world and more loving and compassionate to others.

When we consciously practice the positive act of letting go and moving on, the world softens, becoming less punitive and harsh. Our goals take on manageable proportions and our victories can be celebrated. We stop treating ourselves badly and we look at ourselves and others with tolerance and realism. We are then on course with our own unique life's path.

Sometimes, we work hard on something and accomplish as much as we can—and then find that we can't direct the final outcome as we would have liked. In this situation, letting go is called for. There are times when we are called upon to see ourselves as just one person, one part of the universe. As we stand back and let the universe step in we are free to observe and understand that we have been acting an important but small part within a larger whole. In this way we become more than the sum of our parts.

Seeing yourself as part of something larger than yourself is empowering; it instantly connects you with the awesome creative force behind our world and it reminds you that you are tied inextricably to mankind as a whole. When you give yourself this gift, you are inviting much more joy into your life.

It is when we are connected with others and with the universe that we feel most alive!

Here is the ***summary of the strategy*** for consciously letting go:

Step 1	Become aware that you are holding on to something that is not working out as you had planned
Step 2	Meditate on the fact that you are human and therefore not perfect
Step 3	Look at what you can do to let go of what is not working in your life at the present moment
Step 4	Let go of unrealistic expectations of others and yourself
Step 5	Now set reachable goals for yourself
Step 6	Be patient with yourself and the process
Step 7	Practice letting go; give it over to the Universe
Step 8	In time, evaluate how this new perspective helps you to see the world

Homework

- Assess what is and is not working in your life at the moment
- See if the goals you are aspiring to are realistic and achievable
- Using the summary of the strategy for consciously letting go and the above lesson as a guideline, re-think your choices and see where you need to let go

Lesson 8

Rejoice!

Celebrate Your Victories

Now you have the basic building blocks you'll need to start making changes. By using them and regularly employing the strategies I have written about here, you should begin to appreciate yourself more and feel yourself becoming the person you are meant to be!

But what does growth look like? And how do you celebrate it?

The natural mechanism of growth is a general forward movement. You aim for what you're hoping for— maybe you want your self-esteem to be stronger, or you hope to feel less burdened by guilt, or you want to be able to speak your mind without feeling intimidated so often, or perhaps you simply want to be a better person. As you've gone along, you've seen yourself do some of the things you thought you'd never be able to do. You begin to feel strong and empowered**. This is growth.**

But growth isn't just about moving forward. When you grow stronger there will inevitably be times in which you fall back. You've heard people using the phrase, "three steps forward, two back" and this is what they're referring to.

Remember — Don't let the moments of falling back worry you! Falling back is natural, it belongs to the process of personal growth and you should expect it.

When we fall back, we are given an opportunity to see how far we've progressed and we can also work to consolidate what we've achieved up until now. Falling back is okay and is not necessarily a cause for worry as long as over time you are moving forward steadily. If you find yourself stuck again in old bad habits then it's time to become consciously aware and use the strategies to get back on track.

If you expect to experience periods of falling back you will feel less anxious when this happens and then, when you've started to move forward again, you will feel strengthened by how well you've coped!

When you do achieve a goal you have set, it's important to celebrate your victories no matter how small they may be! It's easy to disregard successes and to ignore the fact that it took a lot of hard work to achieve them. Since many of us have unrealistic expectations of ourselves, we might say that we have achieved nothing! When you acknowledge that you have reached a goal that you set for yourself, you become more confident and your belief in yourself grows.

What if you *celebrate* what you've done? What if you really allow yourself to feel great about what you've achieved?

Don't keep your progress a secret! **Be humble and grateful** to the universe for the blessings of courage and perseverance. Rejoicing in progress is vitally important to the process of creating lasting change. So, do something to mark your progress! Take yourself on a walk and review with conscious intent what you've done and how good it feels to have done it. Or, share your victory with a good friend: have coffee together and discuss what you've accomplished and how that makes you feel. In sharing your changes with others you might inspire friends and other important people in your life to consider trying new ways of behaving in more productive ways as well.

As you share your triumphs, be sure to keep perspective and to be open to how other people choose to follow their own life's path.

By celebrating and highlighting your victories you:

- reward yourself
- anchor feelings of achievement and success
- recognize that you were stuck and that you are able to make real changes
- build your self-esteem and magnify the positive view that you have of yourself
- sense your own empowerment and open your mind to new possibilities
- build character
- strengthen your inner world
- become a more compassionate, caring human being

When you actively review your success and incorporate it into your beliefs about yourself, you can always revisit these happy feelings later. They are like treats that you've kept waiting— they are there to be used and enjoyed by you. They will give you strength when you are faced with new challenges.

Having celebrated and consolidated your gains, you can remind yourself in the future that you've succeeded before and can do it again!

Here is a **summary of the strategy** to celebrate your success:

Step 1	Acknowledge that you have achieved a goal you set for yourself. Be aware of your accomplishment
Step 2	Think of a special way to mark this momentous occasion
Step 3	Celebrate alone or with trusted friends
Step 4	Use the celebration to re-tell the process of how you reached your goal
Step 5	Stay humble, thankful, and enjoy!
Step 6	Evaluate your victory and sense of personal empowerment

Homework

Think of creative ways to celebrate your victories.

Congratulations. Rejoice wholeheartedly!

Conclusion

The main purpose of this book is to share with you the basic steps needed to create and sustain important changes in your life. In using these steps I feel sure that anyone can become a healthier, more whole, happier person. As we become healthier, we move in the direction which is right for ourselves, the one that leads us towards our own unique life's path.

So, what have we talked about in this book?

We began with a basic understanding of what self-growth is and then, having digested that, we moved on to the importance of awareness. Many people seem to lead their lives without conscious awareness, making the same mistakes over and over again and not understanding why. It's time to move forward!

Conscious awareness gives us the clarity to see what we are doing, to understand what we're feeling, and to focus on what needs to be done next.

In our third lesson we gave some thought to one of our most central cleansing mechanisms: breathing. Surprisingly, deep breathing or belly breathing can help us relax, stop reflexive behaviors, and focus us on what we're feeling and thinking.

Through relaxed belly breathing, we went on to considerations about how our past continues to affect us and how we need to focus instead on the present if we hope to change our future course for the better.

Since the past cannot be changed, we can only affect who and what we are now, ***in real time****.*

Trying to focus can be problematic because we are constantly being distracted and burdened by head chatter and the anxiety that trails behind it. The fifth lesson deals with how to stop all that noise so that we can really focus on being in the present moment.

Once you remove the clutter from your mind and create a tranquil head space, healthy choice making is easier to accomplish.

One of the benefits stemming from tranquility is that we are blessed with the capability to let go of pointless anger, guilt, and unrealistic expectations while celebrating what we have accomplished.

Eight great lessons!

Even though these are basic lessons, they do take time and real effort. This book opens up a world of change before you. By reading it through, you are already on a path towards transformation.

Well done!

But don't keep what you've learned to yourself! This book is just the first in a series that I hope will help you move forward on your unique life's journey. By sharing what you've learned and reading further I hope that you connect more intimately with yourself, your family, your community, and with the larger universe.

Now that you have a sense of the philosophy behind *Lessons from a Life Coach* we are going to see how this relates to ourselves on a personal level. The chapters which follow, called ***My Personal Journal***, are the practical component of *Lessons from a Life Coach* and are designed to help you more deeply understand yourself.

When we become familiar with the themes and patterns of behavior that we tend to use in navigating through life, we will notice those that work for us (our strengths) and those that tend to work against us (our areas of challenge). Hopefully once you have worked through to the end of *My Personal Journal* you will recognize the self-defeating patterns that require your constant attention.

It is my belief that these themes outline the areas that each of us on an individual level have to repair and refine. As you work forward, you can think of your progress as your contribution to the universe. Every healthy change that you achieve helps to make humanity more whole and complete than it was before. The work is done little bit by bit, much like extracting a hidden diamond from what appears from the outside to be an ugly rock. Hopefully we will uncover concealed facets of your own beauty as we go along.

This then is our life's work! May we each be blessed with rich and rewarding success.

This is just the beginning!

My Personal Journal

8 Week Personal Growth Workout Program

The same way that we can build muscle and strength through physical workouts, we will build awareness, confidence and empowerment with this journal!

This is the first volume in a series. I've designed the journal that you're holding in your hands to assist you in your journey toward fulfilling your potential. In this way, the journal supports and extends *Lessons from a Life Coach,* so that you can refer back to the book whenever you need to and then apply it in this journal. As you already know, one of the major theories that I have is that we all have something in us that is unique that we are meant to bring into this world. This journal functions as a workbook and it's here to guide you through the lessons you read about in Volume One of *Lessons from a Life Coach.*

No one else will read this unless you share it, so you are free to say exactly what you feel and know to be true about you. I'd like you to consider this process that you're about to undertake as an exciting exploration. Your work here ought to be free and clear of other people's opinions.

In this workbook you will be able to record your progress, ask yourself questions and move forward. In *Lessons from a Life Coach* Volume One you read about the eight basic building blocks which form the spring board to your future self growth. By using this journal you'll be able to create an interactive surface with which you can put those great lessons to immediate and active use!

Things to keep in mind as you begin your journey:

- ❖ This is a process that builds on itself much like gym workouts do. We get stronger and more capable as we go along.
- ❖ Start at the beginning and work through the lessons, doing a maximum of one lesson per week.
- ❖ Always be honest with yourself since honesty is essential to success.
- ❖ This is your personal journal. At the end of each chapter I have left a space that you can use in any way you would like to express creative ideas that will reinforce what you've learned about yourself. Use this space to inspire yourself! Write poems, draw pictures, put together scrap books, paste in photos, whatever works for you!

Things to look out for throughout this process:

- If you rush through the lessons your potential benefits could be greatly reduced.
- Watch out for self-sabotage!
- It has taken you many years to develop your current habits. Give yourself the gifts of time and patience for you to achieve maximum results.
- Prepare yourself to feel some uncomfortable emotions such as shame, guilt and embarrassment. We tend be afraid of these feelings, regarding them as a threatening enemy to avoid at all costs. However, these feelings are a necessary piece of your process. If you are able to ***shift your perception to see a negative emotion as an old friend*** with whom you are very familiar, you can invite these feelings in, explore them, work through them and then put them down.

It's important to celebrate your victories! With each new step that you take and every completed lesson make sure to reward yourself and acknowledge how far you've come! Lesson Eight in *Lessons from a Life Coach* talks all about celebrating—if you need to, re-read that lesson before you begin.

Let's get started!

It is essential to know that even though this process is about you, it is necessary to maintain **compassionate objectivity**. What I mean by this is that you should try not to take the questions and the answers that you give so much to heart that you end up being discouraged and have trouble completing the work-out. Rule number one is to **always be kind to yourself.** Do not judge yourself unfavorably. You are entering an exciting eight week process, so anticipate that this work out is going to be thought provoking!

This is a list of behaviors and old habits that may be holding you back; circle each one that applies to you:

Moodiness
Social awkwardness
Inability to complete a task
Trouble in attaching to other people with trust
Addictions
Laziness
Trouble maintaining meaningful relationships
Avoiding possible stress/confrontation
Easy anger/explosiveness
Indifference
Quick frustration
Inability to listen to other people
Lack of self-respect
Depression
Anxiety
Lack of motivation

Add some of your own here:

____

____

____

____

List **one challenge** that you seem to constantly revisit:

____

____

____

Can you list the experiences that are the most painful for you (for example: humiliation, betrayal, abandonment, disrespect):

____

____

____

Here's a list of some positive emotions and behaviors you will come across during this 8 week workout. Circle the ones you hope to encounter:

Patience
Curiosity
Commitment
Endurance
Courage
Open mindedness
Flexibility
Honesty
Love
New perspectives
Openness to exploring new directions
Happiness
Joy
Sense of achievement
Wonder
Taking responsibility
Success
Inspiration
Surprise

And finally here are some uncomfortable emotions that you will probably encounter while working through these lessons (the reason I mention this here is so that you won't be surprised by these feelings should they arise. If you anticipate them, you are less likely to allow them to work against you!)

Anxiety
Denial
Defensiveness
Impatience
Self-doubt
Fear
Anger
Defeat
Inconsistency
Giving up
Frustration
Self hatred
Failure
Blame
Confusion
Unhappiness
Worry

Well done! If you like, use this space to creatively express your feelings:

Lesson 1: *Anatomy of Self Growth*

Welcome to the next module of your journal! Let's keep going!

What new insights have you learned about yourself as a result of your answers in the introductory module to this journal work book? Write about what you've learned here:

If you're having trouble answering this right now, don't worry, just keep going. Don't fall into the trap of being judgmental or unkind to yourself!

How well do you think you know yourself? Circle the number that fits you best for now:

1---------------------3--------------------5-----------------------7------------------------10

Not at all A little bit Somewhat Fairly well Very well

Describe your childhood in one sentence:

Do you remember the short story about the sapling in a container that it had outgrown? In that story, we learned that no matter how much sun, fertilizer, water or attention that sapling gets, it will still fail to grow unless it is transplanted and given space to spread its roots. By working in this journal, you are transplanting yourself and giving yourself the chance to spread out, grow fresh parts of yourself and really shine!

We all come into the world with inborn character traits, many of which are positive. What are yours? Here is a list to choose some from and spaces below to fill in some more:

Playful	Serious
Curious	Light-hearted
Shy	Humorous
Outgoing	Sensitive
Sunny outlook	Giving
Friendly	Open
Energetic	Trusting
Kind	Warm
Happy	Loving
Generous	Practical
Studious	

____

____

____

Did you understand what the concept, "web of information" means? (If not, the next set of questions will be helpful or you may want to go back to Chapter 1 to refresh your understanding)

Yes No I'm not sure

Here are some questions that will help you get started on bringing into your conscious awareness your "web of information" (you can write "yes" or "no" next to each):

1. Was the atmosphere in your childhood home positive?
2. Were your parents happy together?
3. Were your parents nice to be around?
4. Did your parents tell you good things about yourself?
5. Did your family spend a lot of time with extended family?
6. Were your parents proud of you most of the time?
7. Did you learn to like yourself?
8. Was your childhood fun and happy?
9. Were you taught about fairness and justice in your home?
10. Were the people in your family supportive of you?
11. Did you learn to respect yourself?
12. Did you believe you were worthy?
13. Did you feel you're a good person?
14. Was feeling guilty a rare thing in your household?
15. Was abusiveness a rarity in your childhood?

Can you identify what you've brought into your adulthood from your childhood? I've given you some examples below to take you through it. Review these and then write in some of your own:

Positive	**Negative**
I learned to be sociable	I don't feel comfortable with people
I know how to enjoy life	I don't deserve to enjoy myself
I feel good about myself	I lack confidence
I learned to respect people	I don't have strong friendships
I learned to share	I hoard things/hold myself back
I learned to be joyful	I'm angry
I learned to be open	I am defensive
______________________	______________________
______________________	______________________
______________________	______________________

Now, can you describe what your "web of information" looks like? Write about it here:

____

____

____

Have you experienced a traumatic event?

Yes No I'm not sure

Describe this event in two sentences and no more (write it down and then let's move on):

____

____

____

Do you find it hard to let go of this event or its effects on you?

Yes No I'm not sure

If so, can you identify why you're holding on?

Yes No I'm confused/don't know

If these questions are too uncomfortable for you right now, move on and try to come back to it at a later stage or you can choose to simply leave them unanswered. I know that this can be a particularly painful area to deal with so take it at your own pace. ☺

A note from your Life Coach:

People tend to be ashamed and embarrassed when they cry. However a good cry can cleanse and heal our inner world. It has the power to release emotional blockages that we may have been holding onto for a long time. This letting go helps us to move forward once more.

If you *can* look at this traumatic past event now, what did you learn from it? Using the space below, write or draw about it or use any other artistic resources you like to express your feelings:

Was the exercise above helpful to you in lessening your pain and trauma?

Yes No I'm not sure

Identify the negative emotions that cause you discomfort. Remember that these feelings about yourself *do not define* who you are. Here are some examples; circle those that apply to you:

Anxiety
Failure
Fearfulness
Anger
Rage
Shame
Stupidity
Loneliness
Inadequacy
Guilt

Add any others that fit you for now:

____

____

____

____

____

____

____

Now we're going to look at something new! If you're feeling stuck let's try to find out why.

Can you identify one area in your life in which you feel stuck? Write about that here:

Complete this sentence:
I have constant feelings of dissatisfaction when…

After completing the above exercise, can you note one personal issue (e.g., self-defeating behaviors, social awkwardness, unwillingness to move out of an old comfort zone) that keeps getting in your way and stops you from succeeding? Describe it here in a creative way that expresses how you feel:

Helpful reminders:

1.

2.

3.

4.

5.

Anatomy of the Soul Homework

Did you do the homework suggested for this chapter?

Yes No Parts of it

How did you feel about this question about having done/not done your homework?

Good
Bad
Ashamed
Like a failure
Proud
Amazed
Confused
Surprised
Clearer
Worried
Upset
Excited

____

____

If you didn't do all of the homework, a natural reaction might be to feel bad about yourself. Don't go there! Simply stay with this chapter a little longer until you have the opportunity to finish up the homework.

In Lesson One, I suggested a strategy that you could try to help you become less judgmental.

What places did you go to make your observations? (For example: I observed people at home, at the mall, at an internet café):

______________________ ______________________ ______________________

Fill in this blank: I thought:______________________________________ about the people I was observing.

I was generally kind/harsh in my assessments (circle one choice).

When I placed myself in another person's shoes for a moment, I felt ________________
____

When I substituted kindness, I felt _______________about the people I was observing.

From this exercise I learned the following:

____

____

____

The things in me that pop up when I'm observing other people that I would like to change include:

____

____

____

List the things you will retain, polish and practice in order to be less judgmental of others:

____

____

____

____

____

____

Evaluate the changes that you've noticed in yourself as a result of doing this exercise:

____

____

____

Are you still as critical of yourself? Yes No Not sure

You've finished Lesson One of the workbook! **Well done!** Now it's time to celebrate your victory. If you need to, review chapter eight from *Lessons from a Life Coach* to reacquaint yourself with why celebrating is so important. I'm going to remind you to be sure to honor yourself every time you successfully complete a lesson.

Helpful Reminders:

1)

2)

3)

4)

5)

Lesson 2: *Awareness and Clarity*

Great start! And now we go on to Lesson Two!

How often do you think (and by that I mean make decisions, select choices, come to conclusions) emotionally rather than intellectually?

1……………………………………5…………………………………………10
Sometimes Often Always

Do you believe you have control over your thinking? Yes No Maybe

What does to 'create a space' or 'step back' mean to you? (If you need to, go back to the beginning of Lesson Two in *Lessons from a Life Coach* to refresh your memory with regard to these concepts.) Write your ideas here:

____

____

____

____

Look at the personal boundaries you place around yourself. Are they healthy?

Yes No I'm not sure

Do the boundaries you set up help you or get in your way? Discuss your feelings about this here:

____

____

____

Try to answer the following off the top of your head:

Are you aware of your personal space?	Yes	No
Do you let other people into your personal space easily?	Yes	No
Do you allow too much intimacy too soon?	Yes	No
Do you block people so that they can't get close to you?	Yes	No
Do you give easily of yourself?	Yes	No
Do you allow people to take advantage of you?	Yes	No
Do you think your boundaries are appropriate?	Yes	No

Meditate on the following:

*Sometimes my emotions get out of control before I know it.
*I often react without thinking first.
*I am not always able to manage my emotions.

Do you want to develop skills to help you become more aware of other ways to respond before you automatically react?

Yes No I'm not sure

Make a list of your emotional triggers (by that I mean events that spark an instant, unconsciously based response like anxiety or anger). Here are some examples of emotional triggers, circle those that apply to you and then add some of your own:

I'm made to feel stupid
I feel someone is disrespectful to me
I'm ignored
I'm anxious/stressed out
I'm being manipulated
I feel guilty
I feel embarrassed
I'm sad/lonely
Someone I love is thoughtless
I'm jealous
I feel helpless or powerless

____

____

____

____

Describe a time when you acted without thinking things through first ________________

____

____

____

Did you experience a good or bad outcome?

1	3	5	7	10
It was a disaster	It was pretty bad	It was okay	It was good	It was great!

Did you regret what happened or were you pleased?

I felt bad I felt okay with it I was really happy

When was the last time that you purposely took the time to think first before you reacted (this would mean that you gave yourself a conscious space in which to consider your response first)? Write about that experience here:

Acknowledge your personal growth! You now have the tools to powerfully take control of your own reactions! You are beginning to make healthy choices.

Awareness and Clarity Homework

How did the homework to achieve awareness go?

Not very well Okay Good Great!

Were you able to use the concept of "what belongs to me" versus "what belongs to others"?

Yes No I'm not sure

Did you observe yourself getting involved in things that did not belong to you?

Yes Sometimes Not really No

How does it feel to place ownership where it belongs? Creatively express your answer:

What responses did you notice in the other person when you tried out your new ways of reacting? I've started a list below; add some of your own observations:

Confusion
Surprise
Rejection
Disgust
Pleasure
Silence
Frustration
Acceptance
Resistance

____

____

Can you now sometimes take conscious control of your thoughts and how you choose to react?

Yes No Not sure

List the things that worked for you from this lesson:

____

____

____

Keep the things from this lesson that worked for you and jettison the things that didn't.

Continue to build on the things that work for you.

Helpful reminders:

1.

2.

3.

4.

5.

Celebrate your victory now that you have now worked through a quarter of your workout!

Lesson 3: Belly Breaths

Onwards! Happy to see you here! Let's keep going!

Did you try to do the belly breathing exercise?

Yes No Sometimes

How did it feel? Circle every one of the following that fits with your experience:

Helpful
Relaxing
Comforting
Annoying
Stressful
Useful

Do you think that this can be a useful tool to help you reduce nervousness and anxiety?

Yes No Maybe

Did it help you find some clarity?

Yes No Sometimes

If not do you want to: keep trying to **master the breath** or **move on**? (circle one)

How do you usually respond to anger? Use this space to express your feelings here:

☞ Next time you become aware that you're becoming angry *immediately* try this breathing technique.

After you've used belly breathing review how it felt:

____

The Gift of Breath Homework

Did you get an opportunity to use the belly breathing technique this week?

Yes No

If not, it's okay to work at your own pace. **There's no rush. Don't give up!** Give yourself another week to get familiar with this technique.

List the benefits that you experienced:

Any disadvantages?

☞ Keep practicing until you learn to automatically use the breath to relax and de-stress. Let it become a regular tool in your backpack of coping strategies.

Helpful reminders:

1.

2.

3.

Don't forget to celebrate! You're doing so well!

Lesson 4: *Past, Present and Future*

You're half way through your workout! You're doing amazing! Stick with it!

Do you believe that things that happened in your past are out of reach?

Yes No Maybe

Do you feel stuck in your past?

Yes No Sometimes I'm not sure

If you do feel stuck in your past, write a little about that here:

____

____

____

Meditate on this statement:

The past itself cannot be changed
but we can perceive it differently in the present.

When you mediated on the statement in the box above, what were your thoughts?

____

____

____

What would it be like to free yourself from your past?

Amazing
Scary
Unreal
Liberating
Like being reborn
Thrilling
Unwanted---I like my past!
Productive
Sickening
Calming
Boring
Natural
I don't get it!

Do you agree with this statement: I don't deserve to be free of my past:

Yes No Maybe

If you've answered "Yes" or "Maybe" write a little about why you feel that way here:

____

____

____

Do you understand the concept of "reframing"?

Yes No Kind Of

If you answered, "Yes" or "Kind of", go on to the following questions.

If you answered "No", try to go back to Lesson Four in *Lessons from a Life Coach* and reread the section on reframing so that you can continue with this exercise:

List one example in which you were able to change the way you perceived a situation (that is, how you reframed it):

____

____

____

____

____

Do you want to work on the issues that challenge you most or would you rather let things stay as they are?

I want to make changes I'm not sure I think I'd rather let things be

Many of us suffer from self-defeating patterns of behavior. These behaviors can become entrenched in our lives so that it becomes difficult to overcome them. With awareness, we can choose new ways to behave that are healthier and more constructive. Then, we can move forward toward becoming who we are meant to be in the world.

Here are some examples of self-defeating behaviors (circle what applies to you and then write in some of your own):

Self-sabotage
Avoiding commitment
Setting up road blocks
Procrastination
Obsessing

____

____

____

____

Do these patterns of self-defeating behavior cause you pain?

Yes No Sometimes

- **I am not suggesting you change your personality, but instead that you change the things that have up until now prevented you from expressing yourself in this world in the most genuine way**

In order to change these old habitual destructive behaviors, we need to prepare ourselves to behave differently in the future. Note down the things that you need to change about your behavior that will inspire you to respond in a more constructive way.

Old Self Destructive Behavior	***New Constructive Response***
Example 1: Getting angry/frustrated quickly	Consciously practice patience
Example 2: Feeling anxious	Use belly breathing technique
1.	
2.	
3.	
4.	
5.	
6.	

Remember: I have the power to change the things that are stopping me from actualizing my full potential in this world.

Do you believe that the above statement is true for you?

Yes No I'm not sure

The next few questions are a bit more difficult and more sophisticated. Take your time with them and try not to feel frustrated if you can't answer them right away. You might want to come back to this later on.

Here we go:

If you are able to, imagine that you were placed into your family for a particular reason. What do you think that reason would that be?

To ease your understanding of this question here are a few examples:

1. Woman A is raised in a violent household in which she feels everything is unfair. She is too young and too fragile, as a child, to stand up for herself or to change things. When she grows up, she becomes an advocate for justice for underprivileged people.

2. Woman B is raised in a family in which her brother is seen as the favorite in the family. She feels that she can't compete with him and even if she does "beat" him in certain areas, it's not acknowledged. This is painful for her and she learns empathy. She grows up to care more about others and works with them in groups to help them to achieve their greatest potential.

3. Man C grows up in a family in which he is the scapegoat. He is constantly ignored, belittled and made fun of in order to elevate and amuse his siblings. He grows up to feel anxious, guilty and depressed. He learns to channel the effects of his experience into a personality marked by humility, kindness and generosity. He expresses his childhood pain through music, which profoundly uplifts others.

I hope these examples make it a little easier to identify some of the most basic challenges that took shape for you within your family dynamic. Write now about why you think you were placed into your particular family:

____

____

____

____

____

Write down a list of childhood assumptions you absorbed as a child. For example, Woman B (above) assumed that she can't be victorious even if she wins a race.

____

____

____

____

____

Now, let's go on to the next subject. Let's challenge those old childhood assumptions by reframing the untrue core beliefs behind them. These untrue core beliefs tend to translate into statements about yourself, like:

"I am a loser"
"I am stupid"
"I don't deserve"
"I'm the only one who matters"
"There's something wrong with me"
"I'm entitled"
"I don't belong"

List your untrue core beliefs below:

____

____

____

____

How have these untrue core beliefs kept you shackled to self-defeating behaviors? For example, the person who can't win avoids every kind of competition, the person who can't stand up for herself runs away from confrontation. Write yours here:

____

____

____

____

____

What mistakes do you tend to repeat over and over?

____

____

____

____

____

- The purpose of recognizing your untrue core beliefs is so that you can use them, putting them to work for you rather than against you. Knowing your untrue core beliefs can be life changing!

Do you believe that in the present we have the greatest power to consciously change our circumstances?

Yes No Maybe

Can you think of ways to change your circumstances for the better? Discuss those ideas here:

After answering these questions, do you feel you're getting to know yourself a little better?

Yes No I'm not sure

Describe how you are feeling at this point in your personal growth work-out:

Describe what's been easiest for you to accomplish and what's been hardest in this workout so far. Here's a creative space for you to express your feelings:

I'd like to check in here with you for a moment and see where you're at so let me just say:

The concepts in this lesson require **deep emotional introspection**. You might need more time to process the information in this chapter before you move on. If you feel no different than before, be kind to yourself and stay with this lesson for another week or two, but no longer than that – you do not want to get stuck here! Keep moving-- you can return to this lesson later if you choose to.

Past, Present and Future Homework

Have you found that the homework has been helpful for you?

Yes No Sometimes

If you've been finding that the homework isn't reinforcing what you've learned, what do you think is getting in your way? Here are some possibilities:

I don't set aside enough time for it
I lose my focus
I have difficulty answering some of the questions
I lose interest
I have trouble staying motivated
Other demands get in the way
I've never liked doing homework
I think it's a waste of time

____

____

Just a little note from me to you:

- Don't punish yourself if you're not doing the homework! This process will still work for you but you might find that your progress moves at a slower pace. **You'll still get there!** I'd like to encourage you to stay with the homework–because that way you'll get the maximum benefit from this program.

So now let's review the summary of the strategy that I wrote about in lesson 4 of *Lessons from a Life Coach.*

Can you identify where you feel stuck in your life right now?

Yes No Not sure I'm not stuck!

If you've answered "yes" "no" or "not sure", make some notes about that here:

____

____

____

If you find it hard to write about feeling stuck, use this space creatively to help you discover where you're stuck:

Does this place feel familiar?

Yes No Maybe

Can you associate being stuck with an untrue core belief? If so, list the core belief(s) below:

____

____

____

____

____

In Step 4 of the *summary of the strategy to reframe your untrue core beliefs,* when you challenged your old childhood assumptions, what insight(s) did you become aware of? Let's write about it here:

Write down what this insight teaches you about your life today:

Let's discuss reframing. *"Reframing" is when we review a situation and put it into a new and healthier perspective.* Here's an example of how reframing can be done:

John thought that his childhood was terrible even though he had not suffered through any significant abuse or neglect. When he talked about his past, he always focused on events that were negative. Later though, as he applied the idea of reframing to his childhood, he allowed himself to think about the enjoyable things that he had experienced with his family. He recalled wonderful trips to the seaside and fun times on his birthday. He could then reframe his childhood by including those times and places that were positive and happy too without forgetting about the negative times. When John reframed his past it gave him a more balanced view and helped him to feel better about what he had experienced in his childhood.

You can now try this too.

In step 6 of the *summary of the strategy to reframe your untrue core beliefs,* you were asked to try to reframe your untrue core belief(s). What did you discover? What do you believe about yourself now? Reframe your past in a way that is helpful for you in the present:

And here's some creative space for you to use to express more about what you feel now:

Were you able to identify how negative past experience(s) impact your present state of mind now?

Yes No I'm not sure

Write a bit about that here:

Are you able to identify one of the root causes of your personal pain? Discuss that briefly here:

Use this information to continue to behave in ways that are positive, uplifting and constructive.

Create a vignette to describe your life:

Helpful reminders:

1.

2.

3.

CELEBRATE! You've passed the half way mark!

Lesson 5: *Head Chatter*

Here you are already at Lesson Five! Welcome!

Everyone is constantly badgered by seemingly hundreds of unwanted and intrusive thoughts.

I have called this badgering, "Head chatter". Head chatter is very common and almost all of my clients have experienced it in one form or another. Head chatter can be frightening, exhausting and very intrusive. Let's attack this problem and get it out of the way!

Describe how you experience head chatter (that is, what does it feel like for you):

____

____

____

____

____

How often do you experience head chatter?

1......................................	5..	10
Never	Sometimes	All the time

Does head chatter interfere with your concentration?

Yes No I'm not sure

Does head chatter frighten/upset you? (It tends to create a lot of anxiety)

Yes No Sometimes

Do you believe that your mind can hold only one thought at a time?

Yes No Maybe

Do you think you can reduce head chatter to a manageable level?

Yes No Maybe

Have you made use of the strategy to reduce head chatter that is suggested in lesson 5 in *Lessons from a Life Coach*?

Yes No Sometimes

If you tried it, how did it work for you?

1.............................3..........................5............................7..........................10
Not well A little bit Somewhat Well Great!

If the strategy worked for you even a little bit, let's move forward (and if you found it didn't work, go back to the lesson and see if you can try the strategy again! ☺)

Okay, let's go on!

Write down the phrase of your choice that is inspirational for you (It should be no longer than 7 words):

Now, go ahead and memorize your phrase.

Do you have a visualization that helps you focus and use your phrase?

Yes No I'm not sure

Let's welcome your phrase and/or your visualization here in a creative way:

What would you say is the difference between head chatter and hamsterwheeling? If you're not sure, refresh your understanding by re-reading the section on hamsterwheeling. Write down examples of your own here:

Head Chatter	**Hamsterwheeling**
Thoughts are bombarding me	Same thought repeating itself uselessly
Head chatter makes me anxious	Hamsterwheeling annoys me
______________________	______________________

If you feel like you're running around in a circle, express below how that feels for you:

Can you think of an occasion when old issues and head chatter held you back from achieving a goal?

Yes No Maybe

If you answered, "yes" or "maybe" describe that occasion briefly here:

____

____

____

____

Now that you've tried out this new strategy to alleviate head chatter, how do you feel? For example:

Less anxious
More hopeful
More focused
Less distracted
More connected
More myself

____

____

"Each of us is like a gem with many facets....As we work on ourselves, we are polishing each facet and showing more and more who we truly are." Be creative in expressing yourself as a gem here:

Head Chatter Homework

Were you able to navigate the homework?

1	3	5	7	10
Not at all	A little bit	Sometimes	Pretty well	I got it!

Did you have to focus hard to recall the inspirational phrase you memorized?

Yes No Sometimes

If you answered "yes" or "sometimes" could you tell what got in your way? Note that here:

____

____

____

Write your inspirational phrase from memory here:

____

____

Were you able to distract yourself from head chatter and hold that phrase in your mind for a while?

Yes No Sometimes

Describe what you visualized to help focus your attention:

____

____

____

____

____

____

____

Were you able to integrate you visualization with your inspirational phrase? Write about your experience here:

____

____

____

____

____

____

Evaluate: As you worked through this lesson, what didn't fit you? Write about that here:

List what did work for you:

Personal reminders:

1.

2.

3.

4.

5.

If you like, you can stay with this lesson for a while longer until it feels more like a part of you. This strategy adds another tool in your toolbox. Keep practicing ***all*** your strategies!

Good for you! Look at how far you've come!

Lesson 6: Choose Well

Let's begin the next lesson with an inspirational phrase:

In the midst of a storm a tree that will bend won't break.

It's been a while since you originally read lesson 6. I suggest that you first review Lesson 6 of *Lessons from a Life Coach* about making healthy choices before working through this section of your journal.

Okay, let's get going!

Do you find making choices easy?

1..................3...........................5........................7.............................10
Not at all Rarely Sometimes Usually Definitely!

When considering your options, do you take into account how other people could be affected by your decision?

1......................3.......................................5.........................7..........................10
Never Rarely Sometimes Often Always!

Do you tend to make choices that 'take you in the wrong direction'?

Yes No Sometimes

Write about an example of that here:

____

____

____

____

Consider this phrase: *The intellect is more objective by nature.* How do you feel about this statement:

____

____

____

____

Maybe you find that some choices are resolved through emotional considerations while others are made by using your intellect. Write about how you usually make decisions here:

Review the strategy for healthy choice making in Lesson Six of *Lessons from a Life Coach*. Tick off each action that you successfully and consciously used:

1. Did you become aware that you were presented with a choice?
2. Did you dream up the many options available to you?
3. Did you choose the options that were most appealing to you?
4. Did you research the options you selected?
5. Did you analyze (or research) the data about those options?
6. What feelings came up for you?
7. Did you design a step by step plan to actualize your vision?
8. Did you put your plan into action?
9. Did you give your plan time to unfold?
10. Did you evaluate?

Summarize your evaluation here:

Note: Bear in mind that it is important to be *flexible* which means that you might need to readjust your plan as you go along.

Can you recall a time when a decision felt so right, that the path ahead of you became crystal clear?

Yes No Not Sure

How did it feel when you knew that you had made the right choice? Note down your feelings and reactions here:

____

____

____

A short term choice is one that will affect you for about the next three to six months. List a few short term choices you're faced with right now:

1. ____________________

2. ____________________

3. ____________________

List two long term choices (a choice that will affect you for at least three years and possibly much longer) that you have to make:

1. ____________________

2. ____________________

What did you learn from Kim and Brad's story which illustrated techniques for healthy decision making?

____

____

____

Write about a time in which you had to be flexible about a goal:

____

____

____

____

____

____

____

____

____

Did you work through the strategy for making healthy choices in Lesson Six of *Lessons from a Life Coach?* If your answer is yes, continue on in the journal.

If not, take a few days more to work on this section but no longer than a week before you move forward. If you're feeling bad about yourself because you need more time, don't! **That's sabotage**. Let the process work for you. You'll move on when you are ready!

Are you able to be kind to yourself?

Yes No Sometimes

Have you ever had to put a dream on hold?

Yes No I'm not sure

If you answered, "yes" or "not sure", how did that feel? Write about that here:

How did you benefit from using the strategy from lesson Six? Record the benefits here:

List what did not work for you:

Jettison those things! Keep practicing making healthy decisions.

How accurately do your choices reflect your inner world?

1-----------------3---------------------5-------------------7----------------------10
Not at all Somewhat Fairly well Often Always!

Express your inner world here!

Making Healthy Choices Homework

Now it's time to apply the strategy for making healthy choices to **one decision** that you are faced with now. Using the strategy for healthy choice-making in Lesson Six of *Lessons from a Life Coach* walk yourself through the process:

Step 1 ____________________

Step 2 ____________________

Step 3 ____________________

Step 4 ____________________

Step 5 ____________________

Step 6 ____________________

Step 7 ____________________

Step 8 ____________________

Step 9 ____________________

Step 10 ____________________

Compare what your process is now to how you've made choices in the past:

Helpful reminders:

1)

2)

3)

4)

5)

And now it's <u>really</u> time for a pat on the back!

You've hung in and gotten through *three quarters* of the program---it's been hard work but you've done it----------GREAT JOB!

CELEBRATE! Pick a brand new choice for your celebration—perhaps a spa treatment?

Lesson 7: Letting Go

On to a lesson about freedom and liberation!

Do you tend to blame other people or circumstances for your problems?

1-------------------3---------------------5--------------------7-----------------10
Never Occasionally Sometimes Often Always

When you let feelings of resentment or anger go, how do you feel?
(circle all that fit you):

Weak
Cowardly
Foolish
Brave
Vindicated
Strong
Used
Angry
Free
Happy
Released

____

____

Can you describe what it is about letting go that has resulted in the emotions you circled above? Try to write about that below:

____

____

____

____

____

It is often said that when we let go we free ourselves. Do you agree with this statement?

Yes No I don't believe in letting go

Using this space, write about a time recently when you let go:

____

____

____

____

Do you remember a time when you felt as if you were flowing through life rather than against it?

Yes No I'm not sure

Do you tend to set goals for yourself that are (circle one choice):

Realistic or Unrealistic

When setting goals do you do the following?

Exert intense pressure on yourself	Yes	No
Become impatient with the process	Yes	No
Rush though the process	Yes	No
Feel stressed out	Yes	No
Feel frustrated	Yes	No
Feel disappointed	Yes	No
Look forward	Yes	No
Feel excited	Yes	No
Expect success	Yes	No

Can you say that you have ever successfully achieved an important goal?

Yes No Not Sure

Describe an important project in which you put in as much effort possible toward a goal and then had to let it go:

How did it feel to have to let a pet project go (circle those that fit for you):

Freed
Disappointing
Like a huge relief
Sad
Like a failure
Accepting
Ready to try again later
Foolish
Like I wasted time
I learned a lot from it
Add your own experiences here:

Sometimes you let something go but only temporarily. When you pick that project up again you may be more ready to make it flourish. Has that happened to you?

Yes No Maybe

If you answered, "yes" or "maybe", address the following question:

Taking time and process into consideration, what was the ultimate outcome of that project and how long did it take to see results?

What have you learned from this exercise that will help you attain realistic, achievable results in the future?

Let's segue into a new but related topic:

Do you tend to have unrealistic expectations of significant others in your life?

1------------------------3---------------------5-------------------------7------------------------10

Never	Occasionally	Sometimes	Often	Always

Do you believe: "If my spouse/child/boss/parent would only change how they behave, I would be happy"?

Yes No Maybe

Do you believe that your happiness depends upon another person(s)?

Yes No I don't want to believe it!

Who are you thinking of right at this moment?

Do you believe that you're the only person who has the power to change the things that are blocking your personal growth?

Yes No Maybe

Do you believe that you have the power to change the things that are blocking another person's growth?

Yes No I'd like to!

Assume for a moment that only we have the power to change the things about ourselves that are stopping us from expressing our true selves in this world.

What's stopping you from expressing your true self in the world?

Here are some examples:

- Not staying with the process
- Lack of belief in myself
- Feeling afraid of change
- Worrying about the effects on the people around me
- Avoiding confrontation
- Uncomfortable with the idea that I can be powerful
- I just don't believe that I can succeed
- I like things the way they are

List some of your own reasons here:

- ____
- ____
- ____
- ____

Let's talk about this for a moment. Now that you're more aware of what has been stopping you, you can anticipate that these same issues might get in your way again in the future. The work that you've put into this journal means that you now have a number of very effective tools to avoid remaking old mistakes. You're empowered to put down your defensive mechanisms and move on!

Here's some creative space to use as you like:

Letting Go Homework

Meditate on this statement:

Only I have the power to change the things that are stopping me from actualizing my full potential in this world.

Do you agree with this statement:

Yes No I'm not sure

Did you try to work through the strategy in Lesson 7 for consciously letting go?

Yes No I tried but couldn't

If not, be kind to yourself and work through it in the next couple of days but no longer than a week. It might take more time to integrate this technique.

When you did the meditation on how we are human and not perfect, what came to mind for you? Here are some possibilities:

I think that some people are perfect
I still need to believe that my spouse/parent/child can do no wrong
I'm proud to be a perfectionist
I don't want to accept my imperfections
It's okay to be human and make mistakes
When I make mistakes I feel stupid/foolish/inadequate/inept
I'm bound to make mistakes and I'll try to learn from them

Write more about your thoughts here:

____

____

____

____

In Lesson 7 of *Lessons of a Life Coach* I listed a summary of the strategy for consciously letting go. Step 3 asked you to look at what you can do to let go of what's not working in your life. Were you able to figure out what was not working?

Yes No Maybe

List your ideas of what hasn't been working:

____

____

____

____

Did you discover that your expectations of others were sometimes unrealistic?

Yes No Not Sure

Were you able to set a reachable goal for yourself?

Yes No Maybe

When you evaluated your new perspective of yourself and others (this is your world view) what did you learn?

____

____

____

____

Use this space to explore what you've discovered:

Helpful reminders:

1.

2.

3.

4.

5.

Well done! You should really feel proud of your achievements!

CELEBRATE YOUR VICTORIES!

Lesson 8: *Rejoice*

Congratulations! You've almost completed the eight week workout!

People tend to obsess about their failures while ignoring and minimizing their successes. Does this apply to you?

Yes No Sometimes

If you've answered "yes" or "sometimes" describe an example of when you've done that here:

____

____

____

____

____

____

Do you feel like you have grown after working your way through *Lessons from a Life Coach* and this accompanying journal? Let's review the main points from each lesson; tick off which of the following you feel you've accomplished:

From Lesson 1: Do you understand more clearly what self-growth is?

From Lesson 2: Are you more aware and do you have more clarity now?

From Lesson 3: Do you use your breath to reduce stress and anxiety?

From Lesson 4: Are you able to live in the present moment more often?

From Lesson 5: Are you more in touch and focused in your thinking?

From Lesson 6: Are you able to make healthy choices more easily?

From Lesson 7: Can you let some things go now? Do you feel liberated?

Through this growth period did you experience times when you felt you were falling back?

Yes No I'm not sure

After you read Lesson 8 were you able to anticipate falling back?

Yes No Maybe

Knowing that falling back is part of the process of growing, are you less fazed by it now?

Yes No I'm not sure

Generally speaking, how do you feel about yourself now? Circle all of the answers that you feel apply to you and then add some of your own:

I've grown a lot
I haven't grown much
I'm happier with myself
I feel like I've still got a long way to go
I'm frustrated with myself
I'm much more empowered
I feel like I've got more choices
I know myself better
I can make decisions much easier
I feel lighter, less weighed down by my past
I've learned to let go of some things
I still hold on to too many negative things
I can relate better to other people
I'm more comfortable with me
I am able to reframe things from my past
I'm more self-aware
I see myself growing and hope to continue
____
____
____

Do you feel less stuck now?

1--------------------3-----------------------5-------------------------7--------------------10
No A little bit Somewhat Definitely A lot!

Do you appreciate yourself more now and are you able to acknowledge your victories?

Yes No Sometimes

Do you include friends and family in the celebration of your victories?

Yes No Sometimes

Are you humble and grateful?

Yes No Maybe

Do you need to practice gratitude and humility more?

Yes No Maybe

We're now close to the end of your journal. If you skipped a strategy or have some unfinished homework, this is a good time to try to go back and complete it.

Helpful reminders:

1.

2.

3.

4.

5.

THEMES THAT REQUIRE MY CONSTANT ATTENTION

After having worked through *Lessons from a Life Coach* and *My Personal Journal*, let's assess and summarize what you have learned about yourself.

You should be aware of the "set of issues" that came out of your childhood experience that hold you back from expressing who you truly are in the world. List them here:

1. ______________________________
2. ______________________________
3. ______________________________

How have you **reframed** this "set of issues"?

The one **untrue core belief** that works against me the most is...

"   "

The things that tend to **trigger** me emotionally are....

1. ______________________________
2. ______________________________

The **strategies** that I relate to most powerfully and use most often are...

1. ______________________________
2. ______________________________
3. ______________________________
4. Celebrating my victories no matter how small.

What prevented me from making **healthy choices** in the past was.....

- ❖
- ❖

Now I actively select my course of action!

The **self defeating patterns** that I tend to habitually engage in are:

1. ______________________________
2. ______________________________
3. ______________________________

The **personality traits** that I am constantly working on are:

I am trying to be more patient
I am trying to be less angry
____
____
____

I am trying to **let go** and free myself of the following bad habits and false perceptions:

____
____
____

Personal growth and development is a life time's work. We can always achieve higher levels of self awareness and expanded consciousness. By working through *Lessons From a Life Coach* you have made an excellent start.

Congratulations! Wow! You've done it!
You've finished your personal growth work out and come so far!

A Note from your Life Coach

I feel like we've traveled a long and wonderful road together. And it's just the beginning!

It was brave of you to embark on this journey and I feel blessed to be a part of it.

I wish you joy and even more success! See you soon in book two of the series Lessons from a Life Coach on building self-esteem and confidence.

I would love to have you share your victories with me. If you'd like to contact me, you can write me at: www.lessonsfromalifecoach.com

Wishing you all the very best!

Acknowledgments

I'd like to thank the following people for their invaluable contribution in the writing of this book:

To Dr. Robyne Diller for her ability to convey my vision into writing. This project is an example of how we can become more than the sum of our parts when we join our strengths to those of others. The hours we spent together created a joyful, creative partnership that meant a great deal to both of us. As friends and as a team, we look forward to more books to come!

To Ricci Wolman, marketing executive of Agile marketing for her professional and personal support.

I could not have achieved any of my most important and meaningful goals without the love and support of my husband Alan and our precious children. They know how loved they are.

To Robyn Salkow, my trusted friend and study partner, for her continual encouragement and feedback. She was there when this idea was a mere spark of thought.

Great appreciation to Mrs. Holly Pavlov and her wonderful staff at She'arim College for the opportunity to work with the students who come to learn from all over the world. It was mainly for the benefit of my clients that I designed the techniques and strategies that I share with you in *Lessons of a Life Coach.*

27199532R00064

Made in the USA
Middletown, DE
14 December 2015